The Bad Luck Bank Robbers

The Bad Luck Bank Robbers

The 1961 Havelock Bank Robbery

Grace Barker

Dawn Publishing

Dawn Publishing
12 Friendly Acres Road (12th Line)
Hastings, Ontario K0L 1Y0

LIBRARY AND ARCHIVES CANADA CATALOGUING IN PUBLICATION

Barker, Grace
The bad luck bank robbers : the 1961 Havelock bank robbery / Grace Barker.

Includes bibliographical references and index.
ISBN 0-9696298-2-6

1. Bank robberies—Ontario—Havelock Belmont Methuen. I. Title.

HV6665.C32 1961 B37 2006   364.15'52'0971367   C2006-900819-1

Edited by Gary Long

Design, typesetting, and maps by Fox Meadow Creations
www.foxmeadowbooks.com
Printed and bound in Canada by Métrolitho

Text typeface is Adobe Caslon
PERMANENT PAPER ∞

To all Ontario Provincial Police officers,
who dedicate themselves to making this province
a safe place to live.

The Havelock branch of the Bank of Toronto in the 1920s. In 1961, as the Toronto-Dominion Bank, it was the victim of a robbery of unprecedented magnitude. By then, potential getaway vehicles had advanced somewhat! *TD Canada Trust, Havelock Branch*

Contents

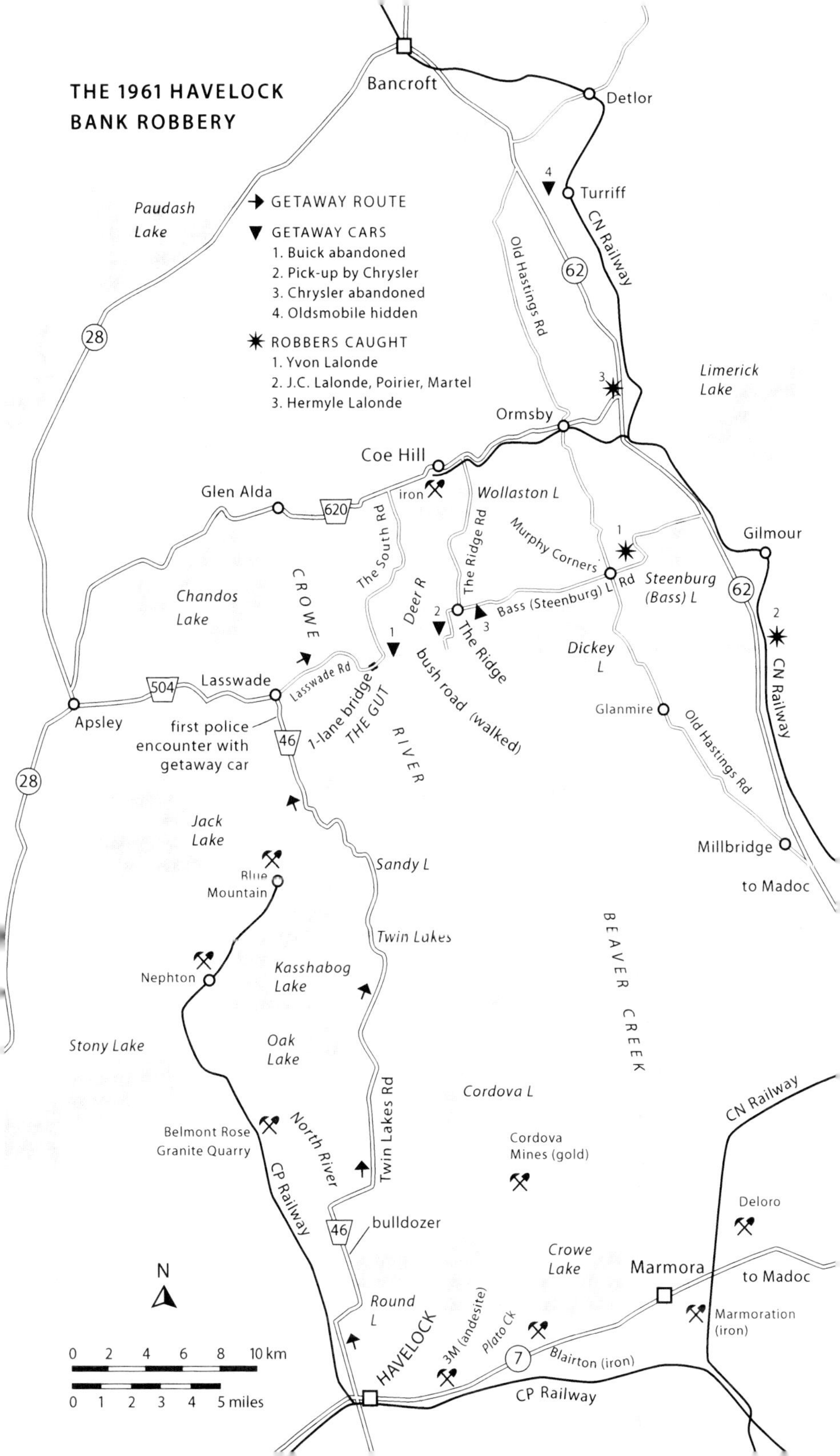
THE 1961 HAVELOCK
BANK ROBBERY
GETAWAY ROUTE
GETAWAY CARS
1. Buick abandoned
2. Pick-up by Chrysler
3. Chrysler abandoned
4. Oldsmobile hidden
ROBBERS CAUGHT
1. Yvon Lalonde
2. J.C. Lalonde, Poirier, Martel
3. Hermyle Lalonde
Bancroft
Detlor
Turriff
CN Railway
Paudash
Lake
Old Hastings Rd
62
28
Limerick
Lake
Ormsby
Coe Hill
iron
Glen Alda
620
The South Rd
The Ridge Rd
Wollaston L
Murphy Corners
Gilmour
Steenburg
(Bass) L
Bass (Steenburg) L Rd
Chandos
Lake
CROWE
Deer R
The Ridge
Dickey
L
Lasswade
504
Lasswade Rd
Apsley
first police
encounter with
getaway car
46
1-lane bridge
THE GUT
bush road (walked)
RIVER
Glanmire
Old Hastings Rd
Jack
Lake
Blue
Mountain
Sandy L
Millbridge
to Madoc
Twin Lakes
Kasshabog
Lake
Nephton
BEAVER CREEK
Stony Lake
Oak
Lake
Cordova L
Twin Lakes Rd
North River
Belmont Rose
Granite Quarry
CP Railway
Cordova
Mines (gold)
Deloro
bulldozer
N
Crowe
Lake
Marmora
to Madoc
Round
L
Marmoration
(iron)
HAVELOCK
3M (andesite)
Plato Ck
7
Blairton (iron)
CP Railway
0 2 4 6 8 10 km
0 1 2 3 4 5 miles

Acknowledgements

No man is an island, entire of itself.

This quote by John Donne (1573–1631) stood out in my mind as I put together this small bit of Ontario history. Without the people who were willing to share their memories it would have been impossible to tell the story. I wish to thank all the people who were so generous with their time and who offered encouragement. You will each know on a personal basis the contribution you have made.

The Bad Luck Bank Robbers is a slice of local history that borders on folklore. It was told to me by Elwood Max Jones. He guided me over the old roads that twist and turn as they conform to the topography of this section of the Canadian

Shield. They were roads that could not be understood by looking at a map. He kept me on track as the threads that make up the fabric of this story were unravelled. This really is his story.

I am indebted to members of the Ontario Provincial Police who offered their help to ferret out the factual details of this drama. Each recalled a different aspect of the event. As I listened to individual stories I gained a new respect for the law enforcement officers in our province who risk their lives in the line of duty on a regular basis.

Inspector Laurence Gartner was with the Criminal Investigation Branch (CIB) for the OPP at the time. He was despatched from the Ontario Provincial Police headquarters at Queen's Quay in Toronto to oversee the investigation of this robbery and was in a position to provide an overview of the pursuit and capture of the suspects. He shared many of the details of this bold robbery with me.

Corporal Bill Baluk was the assigned Criminal Identification Officer for District 8 at the time. His role was supportive to the investigator—to search for evidence, take photographs, dust for fingerprints and to collect and document all physical evidence. Evidence collected was delivered to the forensic laboratory for analysis. He shared his knowledge of some of the details of this case.

Jack McKendry and Morris Baker, who played key roles in this drama, also shared their memories. Donald Lacombe contributed personal memories of the search.

Ed Arnold, managing editor of the *Peterborough Examiner*, gave permission to use the photos and special reports that appeared in the *Peterborough Examiner* back in 1961 and 1962.

But there was a problem here. The papers and pictures I was looking for had been damaged by the memorable flood of 2004. They had been sent out for restoration because of water damage, but when they came back they had no accompanying finding aid. I had already viewed the papers on microfilm and the fuzzy copies that were printed off the reels were not acceptable to be scanned for reproduction in a book. Jean Kirk, who works in the microfilm department at Trent University, was ever so helpful. But original pictures were a requirement for reproduction. And so, the search went on.

To the rescue came Clive Naismith and his wife, Norma. Clive is a retired OPP officer who has recently moved back to Cobourg. He was one of the team players who had been stationed in Peterborough back in 1961 and had been involved in the search for the robbers. As he recounted some of the live-action moments of this chase, I asked if he knew where I might find original copies of the *Peterborough Examiner.* Boxes in his basement that had survived all the moves the family had made during his career with the OPP yielded up the fragile yellowed papers. Thank heaven for pack rats! And thank heaven for Norma who had not said, "Just throw them out." What a find! The coarsely printed newspaper pictures did not have the quality of the original glossy prints made from the reporters' negatives, but they were priceless. Pictures tell their own story.

The library at Havelock proved an excellent resource centre for background information about the Havelock area. Joan Higgins and Sandy Harris were both most helpful. Others who contributed to the factual story were Ray Outwater, Graydon Harris, Diane Mack, Rae McCutcheon and

Helen Tucker. Harold Hunter was generous in sharing his research and photographs. I also want to thank Janice Wilson at Digital Impressions, Cobourg.

Members of the Trent Valley Archives were helpful. Elwood H. Jones, editor of the *Heritage Gazette of the Trent Valley*, is always supportive and opens doors for me. Thank you, Elwood.

Laurence Gartner and Clive Naismith each read the manuscript for accuracy. They offered insights into police activities in the case and did not let me stray from the truth.

My son, Kier, untangles all my computer glitches. My daughter, Donna, and her family offer encouragement for all my ventures.

Thank you one and all.

Despite my best efforts to ensure everything in this account is accurate, some errors may have crept in. The trail of the robbers is 45 years old and has grown cold. I apologize for any inaccuracies, and welcome corrections.

Introduction

On a sunny September morning when Nature had just begun to array herself in her most colourful garments, an old friend, Max, and I ventured on an exploration trip. Our route: County Road 46 (Twin Lakes Road) north from the south-eastern Ontario village of Havelock. Our destination: "The Gut", a scenic gorge on the Crowe River that I had heard about but never seen. Today was to be the day. As well, we planned to check out my friend's hunt camp above Chandos Lake. He wanted to make sure that porcupines or racoons had not chewed their way into it over the summer.

This entire area lies on the rugged, densely wooded, lake bespattered southern fringe of the Canadian Shield. Roads did not adhere to any grid. They just followed the line of least resistance around rocks, bogs and lakes, a constant procession of twists and hairpin turns, dips and dives into hollows, and scrambles up rocky hills and ridges.

When I remarked on the non-level, non-straight pattern of the road, my friend replied: "Oh, they're good now compared to what they were back in the '60s. They were just single-lane then and really not much more than two wheel ruts in the sand. When the robbers were making their getaway, these roads played a large part in their failure to carry out their well-laid plans. They blew their tires and had to abandon their car and take off on foot. It took five days for the police to round them up. They were a professional gang and had a good game plan but they also had some bad luck."

Robbers? Who were these robbers? I did not know about any robbers. What was he talking about?

Just before we got to the crossroads hamlet of Lasswade, Max remarked, "This is where the robbers met the Ontario Provincial Police officers."

After we turned east at Lasswade and approached the bridge over the Crowe River, he shared another piece of information. "When the robbers came along here, there was a car with a flat tire. It was right in the middle of this narrow one-lane bridge when the Buick came roaring down the road. The robbers had to wait until the car was pushed out of the way. The OPP caught up to them here and they had a little shoot-out—just like in the old western movies when the stagecoach arrived at the pass and there was a posse of robbers ready to hold them up.

"This was the third unexpected delay for the robbers on

Author Grace Barker with friend Max on the Crowe River bridge, site of a dramatic encounter between police and fleeing bank robbers 1961. Not far downstream, the river pours through the narrow gorge known as The Gut. *Bill Baluk*

their planned back-road escape route. They just had one piece of bad luck after the other that morning. They must have felt as if they were jinxed after doing such a clean job of making off with the loot from the bank. Luck plays a big role in most things we do and the best-laid plans just don't work out unless you have Lady Luck riding along. If it had not been for these small delays as they made their escape, that gang from Montreal would have been clean out of the country with the loot before anyone knew about it."

Not far past the bridge, Max pointed: "This old road leading off to the right is where the robbers veered off and the police went flying on by. See how the trees hang over the entrance and it looks just like a tunnel. The police weren't aware that they had lost them except they noticed they were no longer following a trail of dust. They backed up and found the bandits had deked into this old roadway. That was an original road when the area was being settled. At the time of the robbery our hunting gang had rented an old cabin off the side of that road for a hunt camp. I was on my way there, on that hot September day, when this entire fracas with the police and the robbers was in progress. On my way to check out the camp that Saturday morning, I was stopped by the police and my car searched to see that I was not hiding anybody or anything in the back seat. If you follow this trail it will lead you out to The Ridge Road. It's not passable by vehicle, and in a ways you have to cross the Deer River. There used to be a bridge across the river but it has caved in and now you have to wade it."

For more years than he cares to admit, Max has been dipping his fishing line into the waters of the lakes and streams in this area. Over the years he has hunted and traversed by foot many of the trails in this wilderness that I was already dubbing "the back of beyond". Max voiced his opinion that "unless the robbers had an accomplice in the area I don't see how these guys from Quebec would ever have been able to map out their escape route with such finesse. It was a great plan but they just had bad luck."

All these comments about robbers aroused my curiosity. I did not say anything until we had paid our visit to The Gut and checked out the hunt camp. No animals had invaded it. We stopped for lunch at Coe Hill. Now put to good use as a restaurant, this building at one time had been the Red Cross Outpost Hospital. Over a crusty slice of bread and a bowl of soup that the chef had named "divine", Max told me a great deal more about the Havelock Bank Robbery of 1961.

The story had as many twists and turns as the road we had been travelling. Since then I have interviewed several OPP officers who were out in the bush that long, hot, humid Labour Day weekend. They all had different slants on how the details unfolded for them, but they all talked about the heat and the humidity, the mosquitoes, the soakers they got in the swamps. And the sweat—sweat that was not all caused by the weather. There was also a spine-chilling sweat that trickled down the centre of your back. And they spoke of their mouths going dry, all the saliva dried right up by the tension of the moment. They spoke of the rush of adrenaline pumping through their veins as they crossed open expanses of ground to check out farmhouses and cottages where they thought the gun-toting robbers might be holed up. This was not just a walk in the woods.

The bank robbery sparked what was then the biggest manhunt ever undertaken in Ontario to that point: some 75 OPP officers in 26 cruisers hunted for clues and the robbers. They were joined by numerous local citizens familiar with the area. Some acted as guides for the hunt because of their first-hand knowledge of the terrain. Many of the officers worked as many as 36 hours without a break. The police officers were thankful to the local people who offered them food. One little girl brought them some ice-cold water to drink. They were doubly appreciative when they learned that the water had come from a spring half a mile away. It was an endurance test but the police never let up on their search, and they did get their men.

Clive Naismith, now retired from the OPP, recalled the conversation he overheard that day as three of the robbers were being transported to the County Jail in Peterborough. "These cops in Ontario don't know enough to go home to bed when night comes. They just never give up. In Quebec the cops would have known enough to go and catch some sleep and we would have got away." Another comment from the robbers was made about one member of their gang who was still at large: "Oh, he will be dead already. He has such a bad heart that he cannot even carry out the garbage."

Five men were tracked down as suspects. But they had to be proven guilty. That was a long story in itself. What about the money? It still has not been found. The Mint has kept watch and says that the bills and securities all had numbers that had been recorded, and that to this day they have never been circulated. The canvas bag containing the loot must still be out there hidden under a pile of rocks. This is a country that has been yielding up wealth in the form of mineral deposits for more than a hundred years. Out there somewhere is a khaki canvas bag containing deposits of a different kind. They are the bank deposits that were stolen from the Toronto-Dominion Bank in Havelock on that late August morning 45 years ago. Will the bills and securities all have disintegrated and turned to dust by now?

Gathering up the details of this bold robbery and fitting them together has been like putting together a jigsaw puzzle. I have listened to stories and I have read the newspaper reports in the *Havelock Standard* and the *Peterborough Examiner* as they covered the robbery and the trial in 1961 and 1962. I have heard about the search that lasted five days and the clues that just fizzled out. I heard about the officer who had the robbers in his sights when the safety catch on the old Stevens pump shotgun jammed and did not fire. My friend Max, who knows this part of the country like the back of his hand, has more than once guided me over the escape route the robbers had taken so that I could fit the pieces together in my mind. I hoped that we would find the buried treasure but, alas, it did not happen.

The Havelock bank robbery was not a spur-of-the-moment job by a group of amateur thugs hoping to make off with enough loot to keep them in beer for a couple of weeks. The haul from the bank in 1961 amounted to nearly a quarter of a million dollars, which in today's currency would be several times that. It was a big-league heist, and certainly not what you'd expect at a small bank branch in a modest village.

This story is too engrossing to be left untold.

The Setting

The village of Havelock sits on the boundary between two radically different landscapes. To the north stretches the vast and rugged Canadian Shield, the remnant of ancient mountains worn down by a billion years of erosion, scraped by the glaciers of the Ice Age, now a sea of rocky hills cloaked with forests and dotted with numerous lakes and swamps.

To the south, the rough Shield rock disappears beneath a mantle of much younger limestone, formed of sediments deposited in ancient seas that millions of years ago inundated the interior of North America. Continental glaciers during the last Ice Age largely scraped the Shield rock bare, but on top of the limestone, glaciation left behind extensive "drift"—stratified deposits of sand, gravel, silt or clay, as well as jumbled mixtures known as till. The land south of Havelock, consequently, is gently rolling with deeper soil, better suited for agriculture.

Havelock lies in the shallow valley of Plato Creek, which meanders eastward to Crowe Lake. The north side of this valley under the village is a long, low, narrow ridge known as an esker. This is a glacial deposit, built up of layers of sand and gravel deposited on the bed of a meltwater stream that flowed across the land underneath the receding glacier.

The Township of Belmont, in which Havelock is located, was surveyed in 1823 by Henry Ewing. The Peter Robinson immigration of 1825 attracted settlers. Five Irish families came to the Havelock area and were the first of 415 who settled in Belmont Township. The British government gave each Robinson settler family of five, 100 acres of land, while every grown son received 100 acres in the family name. Each family was supplied with a cow, an auger, an axe, a hammer, a saw, 100 nails, two gimlets, three hoes, an iron kettle, a fry pan, an iron pot, three bushels of seed potatoes, and eight quarts of Indian corn with which to commence a life in the bush. The government also gave every person over the age of 14 a daily ration for 18 months; younger people were rationed in accordance with age and size.

The surveyors marked out straight lines for the anticipated road network, but the roads often did not follow the survey lines, especially on the Canadian Shield. Trails blazed to important destinations often just followed the path of least resistance, going around rocks, steep knolls and marshy hollows. These trails, which later became the roads, were maintained by statute labour. Each landowner was expected to spend several days each year improving the road that passed his farm. These roads were almost indescribable. In wet low-lying sections, trunks of trees were laid side by side across the road and covered with a thin layer of dirt—the infamous "corduroy road".

From earliest recorded times a primitive road wended its way east to west across Belmont Township following the meanders of Plato Creek. Another east-west road, now the route of Highway 7, intersected a trail that led north from the Narrows on the Trent River (now the village of Trent River) to an area where new settlers were carving out farmsteads. At this crossroads Jehiel Breckenridge set up a sawmill and gristmill harnessing the water power of Plato Creek.

The location of a mill was always an attraction to new settlers. A village began to grow around this nucleus of civilization. It was given the name Havelock to commemorate Major General Sir Henry Havelock, a hero in the Indian Mutiny. The early community was served by a post office, bake shop, general store, blacksmith shop and millinery establishment.

In 1881 surveyors for the Canadian Pacific Railway (CPR) went through and a rail line was laid out on the south side of the road that in 1930 became Highway 7. The first train arrived in 1882 en route to Peterborough's new station. Havelock added a new hotel, livery stable, flour and feed store and even a jewellery store. In 1884 the rail line was extended to Smith's Falls and soon it was completed from Toronto through to Quebec City via Montreal. It was named the Ontario-Quebec Railway (OQR).

As the small settlement of Havelock expanded after the

Canadian Pacific passenger train No. 35 westbound from Smith's Falls, August 1940—arriving Havelock 4:20 p.m. *CPR Archives*

railway came, the new growth was all north of the tracks. It was incorporated as a village in 1892. The original townsite location is now referred to as Old Havelock. Havelock had been made a divisional point, complete with roundhouse and switching yard. The steam engine crews—brakemen, conductors, engineers and firemen—changed shifts in Havelock and many rail workers made this depot their home. They and their families made up a large part of the population of Havelock. The railway was a vital part of the community.

Coal-fired engines belched black smoke into the air as they arrived and departed with bells clanging and whistles blowing. These familiar sights and sounds formed the background pattern of the day in this village. Trains could be relied on. Watches were checked to see if the trains were on time. One could always come down to the station as the train pulled in and see who was arriving or leaving. It made a connection to the world beyond their own small village. The last steam journey through Havelock was made by the oil-fired Royal Hudson in the late 1960s. Diesel-electrics, already used as yard engines, took over. Old-timers tell that this took all the fun out of railway watching.

Havelock had been an important freight depot ever since the 1880s until the service was cancelled in 1967. By this time the railway was no longer a through route, merely a branch line primarily serving local mines. From 1965 to 1990 a diesel passenger car ran from Havelock to Toronto and back, via Peterborough, six days a week, providing commuter service.

In the summer of 2002, thousands of bales of hay were transported over this rail line to the drought-stricken Prairie Provinces. Area farmers donated the hay, delivered it to the Havelock yards and loaded it on boxcars that were sent on their way to their western neighbours. This generous gift from farmers who were already operating on a lean budget was named Operation Hay West.

The Havelock railway station, no longer needed for its original purpose, has been converted into a restaurant. The building itself has been restored and the atmosphere of an old train station has not been lost. Pictures of old engines and early employees adorn the walls and bring back nostalgic memories of days that are gone.

Havelock has always been a gateway to a vast area that had been exploited longer than people can remember for lumber, minerals, and fish and game. Hunting, fishing and a little amateur prospecting has lured many tourists to the region.

In the 19th century, large non-resident lumber companies worked extensive timber limits across this region. Gilmour and Company from Trenton, Boyd Smith from Nassau, the Rathbun company from Deseronto, and Strickland from Lakefield were all busy hewing down the large stands of pine, and floating it down the rivers to their mills. On the Shield, the indentations between the rocks had infilled over hundreds of years with a thin layer of soil, enough to nurture the roots of these tenacious trees. There is a bay at the south end of Chandos Lake that bears the Gilmour name, and a small village farther east called Gilmour. Such place names are reminders of the extent of the lumbering enterprise carried on by the Gilmour Company. The branch railway line that parallelled Highway 62 (originally the Central Ontario Railway) was another method used to transport the logs to the mill at Trenton.

The Canadian Shield rock in this part of eastern Ontario was formed about a billion years ago when even older sedimentary and volcanic rocks were folded, compressed and metamorphosed by heat and pressure deep in the Earth's crust. These processes left them rich in minerals, notably iron and gold, and thus mining has long been an important contributor to the economy. Iron deposits occurred especially around the Crowe River and Crowe Lake in the southeastern corner of Belmont Township. In the 1870s the Blairton Mine on Plato Creek near Crowe Lake was the largest iron mine in North America. Farther north, in central Wollaston Township, an iron mine opened in 1880. This mine was responsible for the settlement of Coe Hill. Small shipments of ore were made from this area but the property has been inactive since 1910. The mine was the main reason for the construction of the Central Ontario Railway from Trenton to Coe Hill in the early 1880s. The line was later extended north to Bancroft and beyond. Now torn up, it was still operational in the 1960s as part the CNR system.

For a quarter of a century, 1955–79, the huge Marmoration iron mine at Marmora, just 10 miles east of Havelock, was an important economic engine of the region. The ore body here was in Canadian Shield rock, but to reach it, 120 feet of overlying limestone had to be stripped off first. The open-pit mine employed some 300 workers at its peak. The ore was crushed and processed into pellets on site, then shipped by rail to Picton on Lake Ontario, thence by boat to the Bethlehem Steel mill in Buffalo, New York. When the mine closed, the excavation had reached a depth of 650 feet. It has been filling up with water ever since.

At Cordova Mines, northeast of Havelock, gold mining was carried on intermittently by different companies over the years after gold was discovered there in 1892. A hydroelectric station at the falls below the outlet of Cordova Lake on the nearby Crowe River generated electricity for the mine (this site has more recently been redeveloped to produce power which is fed into the provincial grid). A small hamlet grew up around Cordova Mines. A general store still serves this small community of people who at one time worked in the mines and who still maintain homes in this scenic location. Rock dumps beside old abandoned mine sites are periodically subjected to reprocessing with modern methods to try to extract a few more nuggets of gold from the mines that at one time had spawned great dreams.

A little farther to the east is Deloro—in Spanish, "valley of gold". This location also held out promise of great riches to be wrenched from the bowels of the earth. At one time it was a successful smelting and refining centre for minerals that included cobalt, silver, arsenic and nickel. Research in alloys at these laboratories resulted in some important new products. The refinery and mine site are still visible today but the area is regarded as a source of contaminates that include arsenic and radioactive waste.

Havelock derived most of its economic impact from two mines that were located in closer proximity to that village. One was the 3M mine just to the east. The quarrying and crushing of andesite ore began here about 1913. The resulting product was used as granules for roofing products. The Ministry of Transportation and the City of Toronto also used it for road construction. Over the years the quarry operated under different names, but from 1960 until it closed in 2002 it was owned and operated by the 3M company, headquartered in St. Paul, Minnesota.

Sixteen miles north of Havelock, mining continues today for the rare ore nepheline syenite. Several quarries sprawl over a 4,000-acre property—the Blue Mountain facility on the east side and the Nephton plant on the western perimeter. The operation is the world's largest producer of nepheline syenite. From the quarries the mineral is trucked to an on-site plant where it is crushed into various grades of sand used in the glass industry. Some of the sand is ground into a fine powder in ball mills for use in the ceramic, paint and plastics industries. It is shipped world-wide in bags and by bulk railcar. The Nephton facility has operated for more than 65 years and the Blue Mountain operation for more than 50. Both of these mines are now owned by UNIMIN. They employ about 100 people.

In 1954, a 17-mile rail spur was built from Havelock to Nephton so that the nepheline syenite could be carried by rail out to the main line. Each day a diesel-electric engine chugs north to Nephton to pick up hopper cars loaded with the semi-processed product. Delivered to a marshalling yard in north Toronto, they are linked up with other trains for transport to distant markets, mostly in the United States and Mexico. A section of the spur line was used when the Canadian Broadcasting Corporation filmed *The National Dream*, an eight-part television series based on Pierre Berton's books on the building of the Canadian Pacific Railway (the series aired in the spring of 1974). Vintage railway equipment was brought in for the shootings.

Nephton existed as a small community for about 40 years. Set in a wooded area near Stony Lake, from 1950 to 1990 it offered modest homes to replace an original bunkhouse for the workers. A convenience store, library, curling and hockey rinks, and tennis courts were added to the complex. Banking and most shopping were done elsewhere.

Another local mine, the Belmont Rose Granite Quarry eight miles north of Havelock., opened in 1965. Granite from this quarry has been sold for buildings and monuments as far away as Saudi Arabia and California. Samples of this beautiful rock can be seen outside of the municipal offices in Havelock, which serve Belmont and Methuen townships as well (the Village of Havelock amalgamated with the two townships in 1998).

Agriculture has been an integral part of the Havelock and area economy since the earliest days of settlement. This activity proved more successful to the south, where it continues on a large scale today, on the glacial deposits overlying the sedimentary rock formations. Most early farms on the Canadian Shield to the north have been abandoned. Centuries of forest debris had accumulated to form a thin layer of soil overlying the bedrock, but after several decades of cultivation it become spent. When extensive lumbering was being carried on during the 19th century, many farmers survived only by working in the logging camps during the winter. Today, one can see the remains of many of the early farmsteads where hopes were dashed and second generation families moved on to establish their dreams somewhere else.

When Prohibition was in effect in Ontario, from 1916 to 1926, many families apparently survived by bootlegging whiskey. At one time as many as 12 bootleg establishments operated in the rugged countryside north of Havelock.

There are a few pockets of better farmland on the Shield where agriculture still maintains a foothold. A good example of this is "The Ridge", standing out dramatically as an oasis of well-kept farms amid surrounding rock and bush about 25 miles north of Havelock. Some two and a half miles long and a hundred feet high, The Ridge is a drumlinized till deposit, an elongated, rounded mound of dirt plastered and sculpted by the advancing glacier on top of the underlying bedrock. Compared to the adjacent Shield terrain, it made wonderful farmland. It was probably this bit of arable land that kept roads open to that area from the north and east to this day.

In its early years, Havelock had no bank. The CPR workers were paid by a clerk who travelled by rail car to the area once a month. The workers were paid with silver and gold coinage, later with paper money. The Union Bank in Norwood sent two staff members to look after the local payroll. Subsequently, the Sovereign Bank established a branch in Havelock and rail and mine workers received their wages semi-monthly. In 1907 a branch of the Bank of Toronto replaced the Sovereign Bank. In 1911 a fire destroyed the bank along with the boot and shoe repair store and the Bell Telephone exchange.

The Bank of Toronto purchased additional property abutting the old bank on George Street, and built a two-storey brick building to house the bank. With the amalgamation of the Bank of Toronto and the Dominion Bank 1955, the Havelock branch became part of the new Toronto-Dominion Bank. Now known as TD Canada Trust, it is still the only bank in the village. However, the brick building built just before World War I was vacated in 1983 in favour of a new location on Ottawa Street (Highway 7), and subsequently torn down. The bank donated the site for a new senior citizens building.

The Robbery

The five men were all from Montreal. They had three cars, two of them stolen. On the evening of August 30, 1961, they made one last rendezvous, probably at a hidden campsite in the bush a few miles south of Bancroft, Ontario, to go over the details of their clever plan.

Three of the men were brothers, Yvon (age 31), Jean Claude (23) and Hermyle Lalonde (36), the latter using the assumed name George Wilson. The other two were Roger Martel (41) and Roger Poirier (31). They all had criminal records.

At some point during the night, four of the men—Jean Claude and Hermyle Lalonde, Martel and Poirier—departed in one of the cars, a green 1961 Buick that had been stolen a few days before in Montreal. The exact route they took isn't known, but as they had no particular reason—yet—to be circumspect, they probably went straight down Highway 62 to Madoc, then turned west on Highway 7 to reach their destination. No doubt they obeyed the speed limit and other traffic laws. They wouldn't have wanted anyone to inspect their vehicle too closely. It would have been difficult to explain the three revolvers, sawed-off rifle, sack of ammunition, and the four balaclava face masks.

Some time in the wee hours of the morning of August 31, the four men in the Buick reached the village of Havelock. Turning right off Highway 7, probably onto Oak Street, they drove one block, then made a left onto George Street. They parked on the deserted street mid-block, near the Toronto-Dominion Bank, facing west. Making sure they were unobserved, they gathered their guns and other gear from the car and made their way to the rear of the bank building. They knew the layout exactly, and knew precisely what they were going to do.

The four of them broke into the building by forcing a basement window. Either there was no alarm system protecting their entry point, or they were able to circumvent it. They were not without experience in such matters. They climbed into the basement, settled down, and waited.

George Milliken was the middle-aged manager of the Havelock Toronto-Dominion Bank in 1961. Like his predecessors, he lived with his family in the apartment provided for the purpose on the second floor of the bank building. During the summer, however, the Millikens stayed at their cottage on

The Havelock branch of the Toronto-Dominion Bank in the mid-1960s, with the manager's apartment on the second floor. *TD Canada Trust, Havelock Branch*

Round Lake, four miles north of Havelock. Thus, during the night of August 30, the building had been empty.

On August 31, Milliken left his cottage around 7:30 a.m. to make the short drive into work. He knew it would be a particularly busy day: it was the fortnightly payday for the CPR employees and for the workers at two local mines, and being the end of the month, there would additionally be senior citizens cashing their Old Age Pension cheques. The end of the month was always busier than usual. There was plenty of extra cash in the bank vault to handle the anticipated demand.

The cash money, as it always did, had arrived the previous day on the 12:20 p.m. train from Toronto. There had been two separate allotments: one padlocked bag came in the express car and was delivered directly to the bank by the express agent. Another locked bag arrived in the mail car and had gone with other mail to the post office, where it had been picked up by bank personnel. Every precaution was taken to avoid a mishap in delivery. The express agent who made the deliveries was a trusted employee. He had received approval from the RCMP to wear a revolver while carrying out his duties. The cash that was delivered on this day had all been new Mint

Before armoured trucks took over the task, cash for the Havelock bank arrived on the train. Here a CPR passenger train pulls into Havelock in June 1950—no money on this one, though. *CPR Archives*

currency and the serial numbers had been recorded before shipment. These numbers had been double-checked at the bank when they were received.

Milliken arrived at the bank building at about 7:45 a.m. He didn't have to go through the bank to reach his apartment. There was a separate hallway, which contained doors leading to the stairway to the apartment, to the basement stairs, and providing a side entrance to the bank itself. He noticed nothing amiss as he let himself into this hall and went up to his apartment to freshen up and change into his business suit.

At 8:15, Milliken went down to the bank proper. Everything looked normal. He placed a pop bottle in the southwest front window. This was the signal (changed from time to time for security) to the bank staff that all was well and they could come in. As an added precaution, one staff member, second teller Keith Scott, did not come in with the others, but telephoned the bank at 8:30. After hearing the manager speak, he came in and the daily routine began: the vault was unlocked, and the staff made preparations for opening and the day's business.

By 9:15 a.m. the manager and the seven other employees were all at their desks. The staff included Mrs. H. Vanderburgh, Jean Kennedy, Marie Quackenbush, Jim Bush, Keith Scott, Bill Lindup and Doug Webb. Just a few moments before they opened to the public, one bank clerk went out the side door into the hall, intending to go down to the basement washroom to get some water to dampen the sponge on his desk. As he unlocked the door to the basement he was pushed aside by four men with khaki balaclavas over their head and holes cut out for their eyes and their mouths. Three

Interior of the Havelock branch of the Toronto-Dominion Bank, showing the vault. It must have been a tight squeeze when the robbers forced all eight staff inside! *TD Canada Trust, Havelock Branch*

carried revolvers and one had a sawed-off rifle. All were wearing gloves. They pushed him back through the door into the bank. One of the intruders shoved a gun into Milliken's back. One staff member was forced to open the vault and it was emptied by one of the gunmen. All the other staff members were crowded into a corner where they were held at gunpoint.

ABOVE "Tellers after frightening experience." Left to right: Mrs. Harry Vanderburgh, Jean Kennedy, Marie Quackenbush. *Peterborough Examiner*

RIGHT Bank Manager George Milliken tells reporters what it was like to have a gun pushed into his back. *Peterborough Examiner.*

TOP Male staff of the Havelock Toronto-Dominion Bank. From left: Keith Scott, Bill Lindup, Doug Webb, Jim Bush. *Peterborough Examiner*

BOTTOM Police cruiser in front of the bank after the robbery. As news of the robbery flashed over the phone lines, press reporters began to converge. When they stopped to ask for directions to the bank, the reply was, "Oh, there is no use to go there, the money is all gone." *Peterborough Examiner*

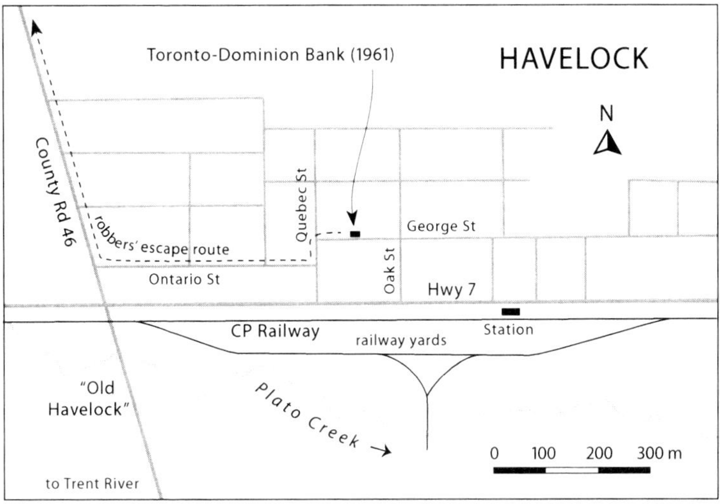

The tills were emptied and cash, bonds and other securities were all stuffed into a canvas bag. The bank staff were herded into the vault at gunpoint and the door closed. In a matter of minutes the robbers were out of the bank. They piled into their green Buick and sped off west along George Street. A few turns through the local streets and they were on County Road 46 at the west edge of the village, heading north.

It took only a minute or two for Milliken to open the vault door from inside. He ran to his desk to phone the police—but the phone was dead! The line had been cut. The robbers had known the routine exactly. They had waited until after he received the call from Mr. Scott, then had severed the wire.

The robbery of this bank on this day had been planned for some time. Over the preceding two years the robbers had visited the area to familiarize themselves with the bank and the lay of the land. It was almost as if they had wanted to be recognized, not as robbers but just as ordinary tourists. They had posed as fishermen and as people looking to buy property in the locale. They had shopped in local stores. They had vacationed in cottages and mingled with the locals. One of them had been noticed attending dances at the Sandy Lake dance pavilion in the summer. This was a gang of professional thieves and they made no mistakes. The gang had timed the robbery to coincide with a day when there would be a maximum amount of cash on hand. It was a robbery that was carried out with great finesse. The robbers had all worn gloves so no fingerprints were left to ensnare them and they had planned an escape route that would fool anyone who pursued them. It was to be the perfect robbery.

The Getaway

At about the time George Milliken was discovering what it felt like to have the muzzle of a loaded gun pressed into his back, the fifth member of the gang, Yvon Lalonde, climbed behind the wheel of a blue 1961 Chrysler. It had also been stolen in Montreal a few days earlier, although it now had Ontario plates, these lifted from a car belonging to a Kingston man. Yvon was probably still at the hidden camp south of Bancroft. Although he hadn't participated in the actual hold-up, he was nonetheless about to play a crucial role in the scheme. Holding up a bank isn't all that difficult. Getting away is another matter. Not only had the robbery of the Havelock Toronto-Dominion Bank been meticulously planned, so had the escape route. Lalonde and his accomplices knew that despite such precautions as cutting the phone line, the alarm would go out to the police quickly enough—a description of the getaway Buick, the direction it was heading. They had to assume it would.

Driving a short distance out a little-used side road, Yvon reached Highway 62 and turned south. Likely he checked his watch frequently. Their scheme called for close timing. The centrepiece of their plan to elude the police dragnet was an escape route along a series of back roads traversing the rugged, sparsely inhabited Canadian Shield country north of Havelock, and a clever switching of getaway vehicles. They had three cars: the green Buick used for the robbery itself, the blue Chrysler he was now piloting south, and an Oldsmobile, which had been stashed near their camp in the bush. These were all big, heavy, powerful cars capable of carrying five men and all their gear.

If the robbery had gone off as planned, Yvon's two brothers, Hermyle and Jean Claude, along with Martel and Poirier, would have immediately driven west a few blocks, then turned right onto County Road 46, the Twin Lakes Road, which led north, quickly leaving the agriculture lands around Havelock and plunging into the rugged, wooded terrain of the Canadian Shield. Eventually they would turn onto a bush road, abandon the Buick, and walk a short distance along the old lane until it came out on the small agricultural oasis known as The Ridge. Here Yvon, having driven in from the opposite direction, would pick them up in the Chrysler, and spirit them up to the bush camp where they would switch cars again, dumping the Chrysler in favour of the Oldsmobile.

Perhaps, depending on police activity, they would lie low for a while before making a run for Quebec.

During the two years of planning for this robbery, they had thoroughly investigated the terrain and road network, plotting what they were confident was a guaranteed getaway plan. And who would have thought to rob a small bank branch in a mere village? But their research had revealed that on certain days, this particular branch in Havelock would have a large sum of money on hand—large enough to warrant an elaborate plan to steal it. Another factor in their favour was that Havelock, like many other small towns and villages, had only a very small police department—in the case of Havelock, one officer, Chief B. Bell (who happened to be on vacation on the day of the robbery!). Policing in rural Ontario was otherwise handled by scattered detachments of the Ontario Provincial Police, the nearest to Havelock being in Campbellford, eight miles to the south. And how adept would the OPP be anyway at handling a major robbery like the one they were carrying out? Until reinforcements were brought in, it would be just the local detachment patrol constables trying to find them. And by then they'd have switched cars and thrown them well off the trail.

Although George Milliken was unable to call the police from the bank, the alarm nonetheless went out very quickly. Even before Milliken could run to a neighbouring store to make his call, others were acting. Ray Williams, the butcher next door, had looked out as he was opening up his shop to start the day's business. He saw the four hooded men fleeing from the bank and wrote down the licence number of the Buick on a sales bill lying on the counter. He called the OPP in Campbellford and passed along his information. The alert went out to all the OPP detachments in the area—Madoc to the east, Peterborough to the west, Apsley to northwest, Bancroft to the northeast, and Belleville, Brighton and Cobourg to the south. This was a little before 9:30 a.m.

As Robbie Burns observed, "the best laid plans of mice and men gang aft agley." The robbers were only about five miles out of Havelock when some bad-luck gremlins got into the act. Some much-needed construction work was being carried out on County Road 46 (the Twin Lakes Road). As the robbers in their Buick approached, they found a bulldozer blocking their path. A delay of several minutes ensued while the roadway was cleared of equipment to let them pass.

George Monahan, a resident of Apsley, was driving south on County Road 46 that morning. Some seven miles north of Havelock, he was forced off the road by a northbound car travelling at an estimated speed of 80 miles per hour. The incident occurred at 9:30. He could see only the driver of the car, who appeared to have a dark mask over his face.

Mrs. Ruth Bovair, a store and cabin operator at Twin Lakes, was travelling north from Havelock on the same road with her husband before 10 a.m. when a car approached from behind, blowing its horn. She turned to look and saw a green-coloured vehicle. Her husband pulled over. As the car drew level she looked into the back, as she thought it must be carrying someone seriously ill. But she saw no one on the floor of the vehicle. She did see two people in the back seat.

Constables Jack McKendry and Morris Baker worked out of the OPP detachment in Apsley, about 30 miles north of Havelock. On the morning of August 31, 1961, McKendry took the call notifying them of the robbery, and providing a description of the getaway car and direction it was last seen heading. Grabbing two detachment rifles—a pair of army surplus Stevens sawed-off pump shotguns—the constables jumped into their cruiser. With McKendry at the wheel, they headed east on Highway 504 (now Country Road 504) towards the hamlet of Lasswade, about eight miles away. At Lasswade is the junction with the Twin Lakes Road. Here they would turn south, hoping to intercept the robbers speeding north. Although the robbers had gotten a good head start, they had much farther to travel and may not have gotten this far yet.

McKendry and Baker were not a moment too soon. After making the turn at Lasswade, they'd only gone a short distance down the Twin Lakes Road when they met the green Buick. McKendry swung the cruiser across the road, blocking the path of the robbers' car. But the Buick kept coming. At the last moment it swerved. Its tail end caught the front of the cruiser, knocking it out of the way. The getaway car continued on. McKendry had to turn the cruiser around on this narrow road before giving chase, which allowed the robbers to get ahead. At the Lasswade intersection, deep skid marks cut into the road indicated the robbers had turned east, obviously at high speed. McKendry swung the cruiser in pursuit. This road, like the others they'd just been travelling, was narrow and twisting, and after crossing the Crowe River on a one-lane bridge, they knew it veered north, eventually coming out on Highway 620 west of Coe Hill.

ABOVE Even the present bridge over the Crowe River isn't very wide; the one at this location in 1961 was even narrower. The view here is east. The house visible behind the trees on the right, at the top of the rise, was known as the Mission House. *Bill Baluk*

LEFT Constable Jack McKendry remembers the Crowe River bridge all too well. *Peterborough Examiner*

Mrs. Dorothy Lummiss lived a quarter mile east of the one-lane Crowe River bridge. She would later testify: "On the morning of August 31st, I left my house to drive another woman, Mrs. Nelson, to her home. I found, however, that I had a soft tire. And when I got on the bridge I sent my daughter back to bring my husband. He arrived with a tractor about 10:15 a.m. We then heard the noise of a car coming at great speed. As the car approached the horn began to blast and an occupant yelled, 'What's that car doing on this bridge?' Two hooded men jumped out and said, 'Get that car off the road and away back into the bush.' They were wearing gloves and one man had a topographical map in his hand. But we could not get the car off the road because of a culvert. Instead my husband directed me as I drove it down towards the river."

The robbers were delayed long enough at the bridge that McKendry and Baker caught up to them in the cruiser. They stopped 40 feet from the Buick. Constable Baker jumped out with one of the Stevens pump guns and aimed it at the Buick. These guns were not always dependable. The safety catch jammed. No gunfire. Nothing! The Buick immediately accelerated, its back window disintegrating as three or four rapid shots erupted from inside. There was only 100 feet separating the cars at the time. Bullets cut the air about two feet from McKendry, who had no doubt the robbers were deliberately shooting at them. All the shots missed the cruiser.

Forty-five years have passed since that day, but the chase to capture the robbers is still vivid in the minds of the officers who were involved. Constable Morris Baker still remembers the exasperation he felt when the old army surplus gun did not fire.

By this time, the Lummiss car had finally been moved far enough out of the way to allow vehicles to pass. The robbers accelerated again, taking off in a cloud of dust. Baker and McKendry dove back into their cruiser to take up the chase once more.

Martel, Poirier, and the Lalonde brothers had not likely expected the police to have caught up with them so soon—and they wouldn't have, if it hadn't been for that bulldozer blocking the road back near Havelock. If they'd just been a couple of minutes earlier, they could have made the turn at Lasswade before the police got there. Now this additional delay here at the bridge was seriously throwing off their careful timing. Yvon would be waiting for them at The Ridge, and instead of being able to pick them up immediately, he'd have to hang around, possibly attracting suspicion.

But there was still a good chance of eluding the police. Just half a mile past the Crowe River bridge was the turn-off onto the old bush road that wound its way east to The Ridge. It was fairly well concealed by a leafy embrace of trees. If they could get far enough ahead, the police might just sail on past, assuming they were continuing up to Highway 620. They could drive down the bush road for a little over a mile, past a hunt camp, as far as the Deer River. The bridge there was out, but they'd already donned rubber boots prior to the robbery so they could wade across the stream. Past that obstacle, they needed only to hike another mile to The Ridge where Yvon would be waiting.

No doubt because they knew they were behind schedule, and the police cruiser was not far behind, they took the turn-off into the bush road too fast. A big, low-slung vehicle with a soft suspension like the Buick wasn't designed for hurtling down rough roads at high speed. They struck a protruding rock on the narrow lane with such force that the car was disabled. Now they would have to hike nearly the entire distance to The Ridge. It was little more than two miles, but the country along the route was particularly rugged. And Hermyle Lalonde had a bad heart. Mindful that the police would soon enough find the abandoned car, they set out down the old lane as fast as they could.

In hot pursuit of the robbers, McKendry and Baker suddenly became aware that they were no longer following a cloud of dust. They realized robbers must have turned off onto the bush road, which they knew about too. They knew also that you couldn't drive all the way through it. Quickly, they raced back to the cut-off. Not very far in they found the disabled Buick. The robbers had fled. Where had they gone? Of course it hadn't occurred to them yet that the robbers might have deliberately pulled into this old road, and were already hiking towards The Ridge.

There was an abandoned farmhouse just off to the left of the bush road. Baker and McKendry surmised the robbers would most likely have run for cover to this house. To approach the farmhouse one had to cross an open field. As the two constables had just moments earlier felt the breeze of the bullets whistling by their heads back at the bridge, they knew the suspects had guns and weren't afraid to use them. It took more than a little courage to expose themselves across an area that offered no cover. Constable Baker admitted to "having known fear that day as we crossed that open field. I could feel the cold sweat running down my spine."

The officers approached the buildings with caution and carried out a thorough search of the house and the outbuildings. The armed men could be anywhere. Behind a bush. Flattened out behind one of the rocks. They found no one. Constable McKendry theorized the suspects assumed that the police would look for them in the house and so they never went there. Instead they had just hoofed it down the trail.

Yvon Lalonde, in the blue Chrysler, reached The Ridge without incident and presumably on schedule. He may have come in along the Bass Lake (Steenburg Lake) Road from Highway 62; or he might have cut west off Highway 62 onto 620 towards Coe Hill, then gone south on The Ridge Road. Past the intersection of these two roads at the north end of The Ridge, The Ridge Road zigzags in a series of straight runs and 90-degree corners west, south, west, south down the ridge, serving several farms; then, as far as car traffic is concerned, it dead ends. The bush road where he was to pick up his four accomplices comes out near the lower end of The Ridge Road.

When his accomplices weren't there at the appointed time, Yvon no doubt hoped they had simply been delayed. Of course if they had already been apprehended, they would never appear. He would have to wait. To his relief, the other four robbers soon stumbled up the old laneway, sweating and breathing heavily, and piled into the Chrysler, Jean Claude

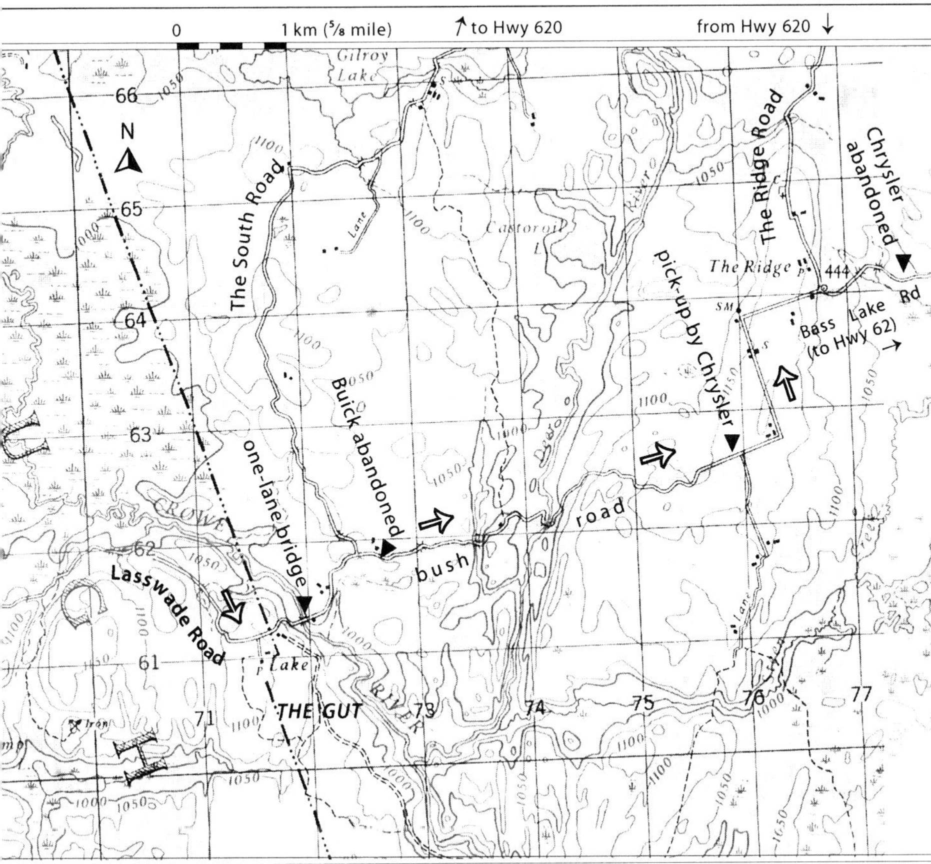

On this detail from an old topographic map, the route of the bank robbers is shown in the area of the Crowe River, the old bush road and The Ridge. In this short stretch the robbers had their confrontation with the police at the bridge, abandoned the Buick, hiked across the bush road, got picked up by the Chrysler, then abandoned the latter as well. The ruggedness of the terrain is evident from the contour lines (at 50-foot intervals)—no wonder the roads are so crooked. Only on The Ridge was it possible to build straight roads. But rather than running straight down the spine of the great mound of glacial till, roads there zigzag along the lot and concession lines, whose orientation doesn't match that of the terrain.

Lalonde in the front seat beside his brother Yvon, the other three in the back—all no doubt talking excitedly about their recent adventures. Yvon put the car in gear and accelerated back up The Ridge Road. They'd just rounded the first 90-degree bend when they spotted an OPP cruiser heading towards them.

Constable Milo Chapman of the Madoc OPP detachment, patrolling north on Highway 62, had received word of the Havelock bank robbery and was instructed to proceed to The Ridge area and set up a roadblock. This was soon after the Buick had been found abandoned, so he was not given any specific make of car to look for. At this point it wasn't certain where the robbers were headed. He was to search every vehicle and every person. If the robbers had continued on foot down the bush road, they would presumably have to come out at The Ridge end.

When he got to The Ridge, Chapman saw a woman walking south along the road. He stopped and picked her up. She was Mrs. Mary Reid, a local resident. Chapman told her about the robbery to explain his presence, and asked her if she'd seen anything suspicious. She said that not long before, a blue car had come down the road behind her, heading south, doing 45 or 50 m.p.h. She'd thought it was her son initially, but it wasn't. The driver, the only occupant of the car, was wearing sunglasses and a pot-shaped hat. He had continued down the road.

At that point a blue Chrysler approached them from the opposite direction. Mrs. Reid said it was the same car and the same driver she'd seen earlier, but now there was someone else with him. The Chrysler slowed. Chapman put his arm out the window, signalling it to stop. Instead, the Chrysler suddenly accelerated past, just inches away, its spinning wheels throwing stones against the cruiser. Chapman had to yank his arm back in to avoid being struck. The Chrysler seemed to lose control momentarily, then righted itself and disappeared over the crest of the ridge.

Chapman asked Mrs. Reid to get out, then turned his cruiser around and set off in pursuit, barking details of the encounter into his radio handset as he drove.

Russell Jackson also lived on The Ridge Road. At about 10:45 a.m. that morning he saw a blue 1961 Chrysler pass his home, going 35–40 m.p.h. A short time later a police cruiser passed. Both cars were going west. After a brief lapse, the Chrysler returned at high speed, about 60 m.p.h, he estimated, with four or five occupants. The Chrysler headed down the "east" road (the Bass Lake Road) and the cruiser followed. He could not identify the driver or the occupants he saw on the second occasion.

Yvon Lalonde was now experiencing the adrenaline rush of driving a getaway car with the police in hot pursuit. He had two choices of route: he could take The Ridge Road north to Highway 620, or the Bass Lake Road east to Highway 62. That was a big disadvantage of this sparsely settled area. Not many roads, at least not ones you could drive a low-slung Chrysler down. The police could easily have blocked both roads by now. The only thing he could really do was go as fast as possible and hope to beat the police. If they could just get to Highway 62, or the Old Hastings Road, which paralleled it, they had a chance of reaching the Oldsmobile hidden south of Bancroft—just 20 miles away now.

Staying on The Ridge Road meant slowing for another 90-degree turn, whereas the Bass Lake Road continued straight ahead. With his foot to the floor, Yvon aimed the Chrysler straight ahead.

The radio-despatched call to all detachments in the area of the robbery had gone out and was picked up by all officers on duty. New information was crackling over the radio waves describing the anticipated route of the escape car. Two other Madoc constables, heading along Highway 62, had picked up the call. The report had indicated the fleeing vehicle was heading east on the Bass Lake Road toward Highway 62. The constables swerved off the highway on to this side road.

Once they had passed the intersection with the Old Hastings Road at Murphy Corners, it seemed certain that they would meet the getaway car. There was no other way out. This road had many small, steep inclines to overcome the numerous hills and ridges. As they crested one summit, they saw below them a creek and a small bridge. The officers parked the cruiser and positioned themselves, one on each side of the road looking down an embankment at the narrow bridge. When the getaway car approached the bridge they would have it in their sights. They had their rifles ready, safety catches off. Any moment now and they would have them.

Up on the great mound of glacial till that formed The Ridge, the roads were fairly smooth and level. But by the time Yvon

Lalonde made the decision to continue east on the Bass Lake Road, the road had dipped off The Ridge and back onto the raw Canadian Shield. Now it was all ups and downs and twists and turns again, with rocks poking up through the sand everywhere along the narrow track. We can imagine Yvon desperately wrestling with the steering wheel to keep the heavy car on the rough road at high speed. Less than half a mile farther down, the Chrysler hit a rock or bump so hard that both tires on the right side blew and a set of springs snapped.

Yvon skidded the car to a halt part way in the ditch, and the five of them scrambled out as fast as they could and made for the bush. Yvon was wearing shoes, but the other four were still clad in the rubber boots they'd worn to wade across the Deer River. The distinctive markings of one pair of shoes and four pairs of boot tracks would prove a crucial bit of evidence in the case.

Constable Chapman wasn't far behind the robbers. He saw the great cloud of dust where the bandits had just abandoned their car. The Chrysler was tilted at an angle, its doors wide open. Chapman spotted footprints leading from the driver's side and disappearing in a northerly direction into the grass. A second set of footprints led from the passenger's side, came around the front of the car and headed north into the grass. Three more sets of footprints were later found disappearing into the bush on the other side of the road.

The two Madoc constables, stationed at the bridge not far to the east, waited ... and waited. The robbers didn't come. Eventually the officers realized that too much time had elapsed. Something had happened. The suspects were not going to show. They put their safety catches back on. Their chance to be the heroes of the day had been squelched.

They would join what was now going to be an exhausting foot search through the dense bush and swamps that characterized the terrain for miles in all directions.

Search & Capture

When word of the Havelock bank robbery first reached the police, following phone calls to the Campbellford OPP detachment, the information was obviously sketchy, but it nonetheless went out over the police radio network, to be updated as soon as more detailed information came to light. Constable Gordon Gray of the Campbellford detachment had taken the initial call. He immediately headed north to Havelock, a drive that would have taken less than eight minutes on the straight road with siren wailing and roof-light flashing. From the information he was able to obtain from the bank employees and other witnesses, he determined the getaway car was headed north on County Road 46. He passed the new information along to headquarters. After the crime scene had been secured and more officers arrived, Gray headed north on the trail of the robbers.

By now it was clear that it was not only a serious crime—an armed bank robbery—but a large heist, and officers from OPP detachments all around the region were alerted and dispatched towards the area; some, like officers McKendry and Baker at Apsley, were given specific instructions as the route of the fleeing robbers became clearer. Events were happening very quickly: in the space of less than two hours the bank had been robbed, the first getaway vehicle had been chased and then found abandoned on the bush road east of the Crowe River bridge, and the second getaway car also chased and then abandoned east of The Ridge, with the robbers presumably now loose in the bush.

At OPP District 8 Headquarters in Peterborough, Inspector Allan Stringer took command of the initial search effort. He was flown by float plane to Wollaston Lake (south of Coe Hill), then taken by police cruiser down to the location where the Buick had been abandoned. By this time many more officers had converged on the scene, both here and on the other side of The Ridge. With topographic maps helping to give a perspective of the terrain and road system, Inspector Stringer ordered roadblocks set up on the highways and many of the back roads north, east and southeast of where the robbers had entered the bush. A search zone of some 30 square miles of bush was established, south of Highway 620 and east from The Ridge to Highway 62.

Corporal Howard Sears of the Madoc detachment was placed in charge of patrol duty on the roads, while Staff Ser-

Inspector J. Allan Stringer (hatless, second from left) plans search strategy with OPP officers on Thursday, August 31, 1961, at the location where the bank robbers had not long before abandoned the Buick. In 1940, Inspector Stringer was awarded the British Empire's highest award, The King's Medal, for police gallantry—the first and only member of the OPP to be so honoured. He was credited with courageous action at Navan Station, when he avenged the death of a fellow officer. *Peterborough Examiner*

geant Stan Palmateer of the Peterborough division had been placed in charge of the ground search effort. Sergeant Cecil Kirkwood, of the Belleville OPP detachment, set up a search headquarters at Murphy Corners. At the height of the search as many as 75 officers and 26 patrol cars from detachments throughout the region would be involved. Inspector Stringer said it was the largest concentration of police forces that he had experienced in his career. Even the hunt for the famous Boyd gang nine years earlier, he said, did not call for the sudden massing of police officers that took place that Thursday. It was a tremendously cooperative effort.*

Also on the scene of the crime and search zone very quickly was Inspector Larry Gartner of the OPP Criminal Investigation Branch in Toronto. The CIB investigated major crimes. Gartner would direct the overall investigation, including the gathering of evidence and questioning of suspects. After he arrived on the backwoods scene, he made his own assessment of the situation. The ease with which these bandits were eluding police roadblocks, and the strategy they had displayed during the actual robbery, led Gartner to believe that they were a professional gang and the Quebec licence plate on the Buick had made him suspect that they were most likely from the Montreal area. Contact with the Montreal police force, which might be able to offer some assistance, seemed a prudent move. He dispatched another CIB officer down to Montreal to see if he could get any leads on who this crew was. The information Gartner heard back was conjecture, but it provided a good idea of who they might be and what

*The four-member Boyd gang (named for leader Edwin Boyd) gained notoriety and headlines in the early 1950s for a series of bold bank robberies and cunning prison escapes in Toronto. After escaping from the Don Jail in 1951, they pulled off the biggest bank robbery in Toronto's history to that date. They were then at large for some time before two of the gang members shot and killed a Toronto police officer in March 1952. A major manhunt began. Rounded up and put back in the Don Jail, the four men escaped again in September. Another manhunt ensued. After eight days the robbers were recaptured—for good, this time—in Toronto.

skills would be needed to apprehend them. There had been a number of robberies in Montreal attributed to the "Red Hood Gang", and it was thought that the Havelock robbery might have been undertaken by members of that group.

As the police uncovered many clues of where the robbers had been, the search area steadily extended eastward. When the trail across from the Buick to The Ridge Road was searched some items were picked up here. But not a canvas bag filled with money. Were the robbers still toting it along with them as they fled steadily towards the east? And what about the guns? Were the robbers still armed and would they shoot at police officers? What they did find was a gun holster of the snap-shoulder type. Marks on it indicated that it had carried a revolver with a four-inch barrel. A station wagon coat and a set of blue overalls were also found on the trail by Herb Moore, a district farmer who was helping out in the search. The clothes matched the description of those worn by the robbers and they were sent to Toronto for laboratory tests. But the robbers were out here somewhere, perhaps with the loot and their guns, loaded and ready.

As the search led steadily eastward no sightings were made of the robbers. But clues kept turning up to indicate where they had been. Each clue had to be followed up. Deserted farmhouses in the area had to be investigated—with great caution. This was a nerve-wracking procedure for the officers who were constantly on the alert not knowing what was behind each door that was opened. On Friday they discovered an area where they thought the robbers had bedded down on Thursday night after fleeing from the disabled Chrysler. Near

Constable Tom Armitage (right) of the Peterborough OPP detachment, along with another OPP officer, question a motorist at a checkpoint on one of the back roads in the sparsely inhabited bush country south of Coe Hill. The road is typical of those the robbers attempted to escape along. The photograph gives a good idea of the kind of terrain the robbers, and the police, had to tramp through. *Peterborough Examiner*

a bed of leaves they found cigar and cigarette butts and wrappers.

There was a possibility that the hunted men might travel down a dirt road to the south of The Ridge that emerges near Marmora. Max, who has been hunting, fishing and cutting lumber in the area for years, advanced the theory that "they would have to travel it during the day as it is impossible to traverse it at night because of the many bluffs along the route." His advice was to "just sit tight like we do when we are deer hunting and wait for them to come out."

The robbers could also make their way on foot in the day through the bush parallelling the Bass (Steenburg) Lake Road, eventually reach Highway 62 and perhaps steal a car there and make their getaway. Or they could have holed up in a cottage they had been occupying for the past month posing as tourists. The police didn't know about the Oldsmobile hidden south of Bancroft. The robbers were probably hoping they could reach that.

Inspector Stringer was asked if there might not have been accomplices near Havelock who could have taken delivery of the stolen money and then made their way off in a different direction. Stringer pointed out that the behaviour of the hunted men was strongly indicative of guilt. "If they hadn't still got the money, all they needed to do was to get rid of the guns and masks. They could sit by the side of the road and ask us to give them a lift." Another thing they might have done was to have gone straight down to Highway 7 and then to Highway 401 and driven along it, rather than north through the back roads. Stringer said: "We could not possibly give all the traffic on that road a thorough check and search.

Taking no chances, an OPP officer armed with a carbine stands guard as other officers search this International Travelall stopped at a checkpoint. *Peterborough Examiner*

We'd have the cars backed up to Toronto in no time." The search went on in this rugged country that provided cover for the hunted men—but also limited their options.

Late Friday night the police checked out a report from two teenagers of unusual activity at a supposedly empty house. Charles Drumm was driving Shirley Robbins to her home near Steenburg Lake, and the two noticed lights in the window of the Robbins house. As they drove near, the lights went out. At once the two returned to the OPP roadblock near Steenburg and two police constables went with them in the cruiser to check things out. As they approached the house, the dogs began to bark furiously at the back. Both officers moved forward slowly, guns ready. This was another of those gut-wrenching moments. What were they walking in to? In the kitchen they found remains of a hasty snack. Four corn cobs lay beside the sink and the kettle was still warm. But Miss Robbins' father had left for a meeting two hours earlier. The find was reported to search headquarters at Murphy Corners, and an inch-by-inch search of the barn, house and adjoining field was conducted, without results. Minutes afterward, it was discovered that Miss Robbins' two brothers had eaten the corn and just by coincidence had switched off the lights as Mr. Drumm and their sister had driven up.

After Constable Chapman spotted the robbers driving on The Ridge Road on Thursday morning, nobody had actually seen them since. Footprints and other evidence, yes, but no robbers. A break came early on Saturday, September 2. At about 7:30 a.m., Martin Murphy was driving along Old Hastings Road, heading to work at a mill at Murphy Corners. When he came over a hill he saw two men on the road. They did not move, but when his car entered a dip in the road and came up again, the men crouched down and ran into the woods. He reported this to the police and returned to the spot with OPP Constable Mel Schultz, of the Madoc detachment, and they found foot tracks. One set was made by a "pointed shoe" and the other by "rubbers".

Constable Schultz followed the tracks but lost them. Then, about 11 a.m., he found more tracks and followed them for a few yards only to lose them again. He finally came out near

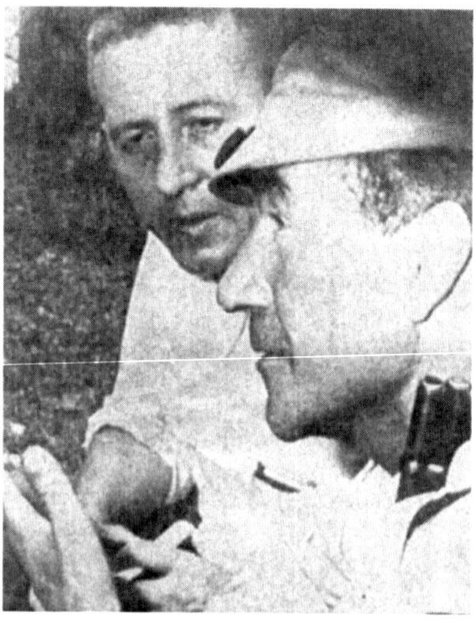

ABOVE Local resident Martin Murphy points out a location on a map for Constable Kirkwood along the Bass (Steenburg) Lake Road. *Peterborough Examiner*

LEFT Inspector Laurence Gartner (foreground) confers with Martin Murphy during the search for the robbers. Murphy was the first to spot the robbers after they abandoned the Chrysler. *Peterborough Examiner* the back of the Curtis Fitzgibbon residence at Bass (Steenburg) Lake.

Around 1 p.m., accompanied by Constable Bruce Shaw, also of the Madoc detachment, Schultz spotted a man under a tree at the edge of a clearing, about 300 feet from the Bass Lake Road. The man was lying face down, probably hoping to avoid detection. Schultz had to order the man to get up two or three times before he did so. It was Yvon Lalonde, who asked, "Is anything wrong?" He was bearded, and wet from an all-night soaking rain. "I don't know what you want me for," he protested. "I was just hitch-hiking and got lost." His clothing was torn and he wore pointed shoes that resembled the outline of the tracks Schultz had been following. He was unarmed. He offered no resistance when he was handcuffed. He seemed to take this in his stride.

Lalonde was taken to a nearby boathouse owned by a Mr. Weller, where he was restrained and searched. His pockets did not contain $230,000. A wad of wet soggy bills were made up of three fives, a two, three ones, and $1.42 in loose change—a grand total of $21.42. His jacket pockets yielded a few small crab-apples and a bottle of water. Yvon also had a key ring with three keys on it. That would prove significant. It was later determined that one key started the Buick, another the Chrysler and the third the Oldsmobile, which the police didn't yet know about when they captured Yvon.

Constable Chapman identified Yvon as the driver of the Chrysler he had pursued on The Ridge back on Thursday morning. Lalonde was described as five feet, six inches tall, heavily built and paunchy.

The second man that Martin Murphy saw on the road had

Yvon Lalonde, the first of the "bad luck bank robbers" to be captured, sits glumly in a boathouse at Steenburg Lake, guarded by constables Mel Schultz (left) and Bruce Shaw, who had found and arrested him a short time earlier. Note his "pot-shaped" hat, as it was described by one witness. *Peterborough Examiner*

Constable Bruce Shaw relaxes and sheds his wet boots after the successful capture of Yvon Lalonde. *Peterborough Examiner*

taken off into the bush and was not found on Saturday. Tension rose as it became almost certain that the other fugitives were close by. Although Yvon Lalonde had been captured without a shot being fired, the officers had fired off two signal shots to notify other officers searching the area that they had found and captured one of the robbers. This had been misinterpreted by searchers nearby as a gun battle. Local residents were hoping that the fugitives would soon be caught. Everyone was anxious.

The bush area that was being searched was infested with mosquitoes that attacked hungrily in these hot humid condi-

Corporal Doug Sears of the Madoc detachment escorts Yvon Lalonde to an OPP cruiser at Steenburg Lake. *Peterborough Examiner*

tions. Police expected that any culprits they ran across would be desperate after spending 48 hours on the run. They would be wet, hungry, bug-bitten and tired. Local residents offered support to the police and supplied them with extra rifles for the Saturday search. Tension mounted. Security measures tightened. Some began to surmise that the robbers had slipped through the net and were already away. But the police just carried on with diligence. Stop-checks had gone on all night long throughout a torrential downpour of rain. More than 100 cars had been stopped along Highway 62 while the police checked drivers' identification, back seats and trunks.

Many officers had now put in more than 36 hours on duty, without a break. Dawn emerged out of a heavy fog that lasted until about 9 a.m. On-duty officers hoped that they would soon find the other bandits. Then they could go home for a shower and a soft bed.

Theories abounded as the patrols and the search continued throughout the night. It was a boring patrol duty with much effort being exerted to fend off the swarms of mosquitoes. In this hot humid atmosphere the bugs were having a heyday drawing blood.

Staff Sergeant Palmateer organized search parties to investigate the woods south of Bass Lake. Each party was led by a

All night through pouring rain, police diligently stop and check vehicles on Highway 62. *Peterborough Examiner*

local woodsman who was familiar with the area. Clive Naismith, of the Peterborough OPP detachment, was teamed up with Tom Armitage (a fellow officer) and Charles Murphy and Bob McGeachie, two local woodsmen acknowledged to be familiar with the terrain. They were armed with sawed-off shotguns and a rifle in addition to their side arms. Twenty minutes into their bush trek their light blue uniform shirts clung to their backs and had turned dark. They were to search the old Moore farm and join up with a party at Fowler's Landing. Communication with the other search parties was by walkie-talkie. If only they had a police search dog. But this was 1961 and the Ontario Provincial Police had no canine unit. Inspector Laurence Gartner had contacted the RCMP, who were training some search dogs in New Brunswick, but it would take too long to get them up here and by then the scent would be faint. The only signs that were picked up on this hot sweaty trek were some spoor left by a bear.

Clive Naismith recalls going to the cottages along the south shore of Bass Lake with another officer. They were letting cottagers know that the cordon had tightened and that the robbers might try to steal a boat. "Take the motors off them and park them," cottagers were advised. Shortly after midnight, Saturday, there was a report that a cottage on the southeast shore of Bass Lake had been broken into and a boat stolen. As some of the police force investigated the cottage itself, other searchers on foot strung out and began to search the woods between the road and the lake. They were led by Inspector Gartner. Nothing happened. No fugitive was found lurking in the area. The search was a painstaking affair, looking under wharves, under the bushes, inside a tent. Nobody!

Clive Naismith, one of over 70 OPP officers who searched for the Havelock bank robbers, later became Deputy Commissioner. *Clive Naismith*

Nobody! The search in that area was called off. Meanwhile, the cottage that had been broken into was checked out. Two windows had been smashed and a quantity of food taken. There was no indication of how many people had entered the cottage or if they had indeed been the robbers. Inspector Gartner issued an alert to all checkpoints. Whoever stole the boat might next steal a car. Police cruisers were to be placed crosswise on the roads as roadblocks.

Residents living in the search area kept their shotguns handy. Here, Mary (Mrs. Hiram) Reid, with gun, and Carol Hoard keep a lookout. Mary Reid saw the robbers driving on The Ridge Road on the day of the robbery and pointed their car out to Constable Chapman. *Peterborough Examiner*

A boat was borrowed from a sleepy cottager. Constables Clive Naismith and Tom Armitage, along with two cottagers, took off across the lake to look for the missing craft—and perhaps the robbers. Suspense ran high. Naismith recalls that the lake was choppy. They were almost at the other shore when a call came on their walkie-talkie from the place they had just left. The voice sounded frantic: "Come back! Come back! There's a man standing up in a boat just out from this shore. He's waving." So they tore back across the choppy lake. As they approached the so-called man, they discovered it was a marker buoy—a buoy, not a man! The chop on the water had caused it to rock and those on shore had been mistaken. As Clive recalls this incident some 45 years later, he now finds great humour in the situation.

Meanwhile, on another section of the shoreline that was being monitored, Inspector Gartner was standing out on a point when he saw something floating in. It was hard to see in the mist. It could be the robbers drifting in a boat. As he glanced around he saw that other men had gathered with him. Good! He had back-up officers on hand. Then he looked again. They weren't police officers, but press reporters! His mouth went dry. He was alone to deal with the drifting boat. But it was not a boat. As it drew closer he saw that it was just an old log. High drama over unreal situations.

A report that crackled over the communication network alerted everyone that a car was approaching a checkpoint with a driver they did not recognize and a second occupant who looked suspicious. The car was stopped. The occupants were found to be reporters from the *Peterborough Examiner* on the trail of a good story (an interesting side note: the publisher of the *Examiner* at that time was Robertson Davies, already gaining fame as an author).

Altogether Saturday was a day of great suspense—and all but one of the robbers were still on the loose.

On Sunday, the tide turned. Sergeant Stan Palmateer succeeded in following some boot prints all the way to the

Constable George Mountsteven (left), of the Haliburton OPP detachment, carries his own sub-machine gun during the search. He created a brief moment of excitement when he accidentally let off a barrage of six or eight shots—another false alarm. *Peterborough Examiner*

Canadian National Railway line near Highway 62. Three men were spotted walking along the tracks about a quarter of a mile away, heading south. Immediately a force of police surrounded the area. Volunteers were enlisted from many of the civilians who had come to the scene. Most were armed with a variety of firearms, such as the vintage model 30-30 owned by Owen Tripp, whose grandfather bought it for $10 in 1912 from a moose hunter in northern Saskatchewan. Some had high-priced sporting rifles. The search was a short one. Lasting little more than an hour, it concentrated in the bush east of where the bandits had been seen on the tracks. The searchers formed an ever-tightening noose around the area in an attempt to sweep the suspects back to the tracks where a line of armed men waited.

Many civilians took part in the search. Curtis Fitzgibbon of Steenburg Lake (LEFT) brandishes his carbine; on the day Yvon Lalonde was captured near his house, he saw one of the other robbers duck into the bush. Fred Andrews (RIGHT), from the Stirling area, found Poirier, Martel, and J.C. Lalonde after they'd been spotted running from the CNR railway tracks. *Peterborough Examiner*

Civilian Fred Andrews found the three fugitives. He yelled at them to stay where they were, and fired two shots into the air—the agreed-upon signal that the fugitives had been found. Constable John Martin of the Brighton OPP was the first to reach Andrews and take charge of the wanted men. These three proved to be Roger Poirier, Roger Martel, and Jean Claude Lalonde. They proclaimed that they had no knowledge of the robbery. Why they had been walking south on the railway tracks is not entirely certain. If they had turned north instead, they would have reached the hidden camp and Oldsmobile getaway car in a matter of hours. Perhaps, exhausted and disoriented after three days of thrashing through the humid, bug-infested woods, they had simply made a mistake. Another bit of bad luck for the robbers!

The three arrested men were taken to Griffin's service station in Millbridge for initial questioning. Hundreds of local residents and vacationers mingled with police hoping to catch a glimpse of the robbers, and to see if they still had the loot on them. The men were hustled inside the garage to await interrogation by Inspector Gartner, who arrived on the scene bare-headed, clad in white shirt and grey flannels with a .38-special on his hip. The door of the garage banged down, depriving onlookers of their "look-see" at the robbers.

Everyone heaved a sigh of relief that the search was over. Inspector Gartner said no, there was a fifth one still loose. The search wasn't over.

But it was over very soon, and after the high drama of the past few days, it ended uneventfully. The next morning, Labour Day Monday, September 4 (96 hours now since the robbery), a northbound motorist on Highway 62 was stopped

Hundreds of vacationers and local residents mingle with police at Millbridge (TOP) on Sunday, hoping to get a glimpse of the three robbers captured nearby along the railway. Roger Poirier, Roger Martel and Jean Claude Lalonde (BOTTOM) have their faces blacked out in this newspaper picture at the request of the police, pending their appearance in a police lineup. *Peterborough Examiner*

Constable Gordon Gray of the Campbellford OPP escorts one of the captured robbers on Sunday, September 3. He was the officer who took the initial call notifying police of the robbery the previous Thursday, and was first on the scene at the bank. *Peterborough Examiner*

at a roadblock north of the Highway 620 turn-off for a routine check. He told of a bedraggled man back a ways near the junction, who was trying to hitch a ride going north. The officers on duty were constables Charles Disley and Ray Hooker of the Bancroft OPP detachment. They immediately drove south and picked up the man without a struggle. It was

Hermyle Lalonde. He told the officers he was George Wilson of Ottawa, and expressed gratitude that they had found him. He said that he was lost and that his heart was starting to give him a problem. He appeared all in and his feet were raw from the rubber boots he had been wearing on his four-day trek through the woods.

Hermyle had apparently oriented himself correctly, and while Poirier, Martel and Jean Claude Lalonde had gone south, he had headed north. In just another seven miles he would have arrived at the camp that had been set up near Detlor. It was obvious that he had emerged out on to the highway hoping to pick up a ride. He did not want to do any more walking. He complained of a sore toe. He did not reveal that he had any connection with a gang of robbers. He was just a tired man who needed a ride. The officers obliged by giving him a ride to the Peterborough jail.

Gathering Evidence

The five suspects were all detained in the County Jail in Peterborough. They made a brief court appearance in Peterborough County Courthouse on Tuesday, September 5. The five were under heavy police guard. Yvon and Hermyle Lalonde were handcuffed together (Hermyle was still being identified as George Wilson), as were Jean Claude Lalonde, Roger Martel and Roger Poirier.

Magistrate W.R. Philp presided. He ordered the jammed courtroom cleared of everyone not seated. After hearing individual charges and a collective charge of armed robbery read against them, the five prisoners were remanded without plea to the following Tuesday. Lawrence Corriveau of

Quebec City, attorney for the five accused, told Magistrate Philp that they would be represented by John Mirsky, QC, of Ottawa, when their case came up for trial.

After the hearing, the five men were moved from the Peterborough County Jail to the Ontario County Jail in Whitby. Inspector J.A. Stringer said he felt the Peterborough jail was more susceptible to a break-out than the more modern Whitby jail, which would offer nearer maximum security. The prisoners would be transported from Whitby to the Peterborough Courthouse on a daily basis for the trial.

Inspector Laurence Gartner had the cells at the Whitby jail wired, hoping to pick up a clue to the location of the loot. However, the prisoners remained tight-lipped and they all proclaimed they had no part in the robbery.

Now that the five suspects had been captured, there was still a lot of work to do searching for evidence in the rugged expanse of countryside where the robbers had been loose. A team of specially picked officers led by Staff Sergeant Stan Palmateer was assigned to the task and spent five weeks tracking through miles of bush looking for the loot, or the guns, or the balaclavas and gloves that the suspects had been wearing when they were seen at the Crowe River bridge. Officers followed the old bush road the robbers had walked in order to reach the The Ridge, and combed the bush east from where they had abandoned the Chrysler. Mine detectors loaned by the army were used as the search continued. Sergeant Palmateer understood these had a range of 40 feet from the operator. Finding the guns, including the M1 carbine, would be a great help. People of various ages from around the countryside were out looking, hoping to be the ones to find

Corporal Bill Baluk, OPP Criminal Identification Officer, dusts for prints on the Chrysler abandoned by the robbers on the Bass Lake Road. He found none. *Peterborough Examiner*

the money. The entire area was put under police surveillance and it was announced out of bounds for other than authorized personnel. "We want no searchers in the area who are not under our supervision and at the moment we have all the help we need," Sergeant Palmateer said. A helicopter hovered overhead hoping to spot some evidence from the sky.

When the suspects had been searched following their capture, Poirier had $41.60 in his pockets, Jean Claude Lalonde $105.00, Martel $134.60 and Yvon Lalonde $21.42. Hermyle Lalonde, a.k.a. George Wilson, had a pocketful of pills to control possible heart attacks. None of the suspects was carrying any crisp new bills that had been lifted from the bank.

And where were the guns they had been carrying and brandishing? Where were the balaclavas they had worn in the bank? The men had left behind jackets and overalls because the weather had turned out to be so unseasonably hot. A gun holster had been found but no guns and no canvas bag filled with the money from the bank.

But despite the painstaking efforts of the search team, no sign of the guns, balaclavas, gloves and especially the canvas bag containing the stolen cash and securities could be found anywhere. The section along the bush road where the robbers had hiked after abandoning the Buick was a fairly compact area to search, as the four fugitives wouldn't have had time to stray far from the road in their haste to reach The Ridge. However, after they abandoned the Chrysler, the robbers had walked for dozens of miles, not always together, through a vast tract of bush with numerous swamps, beaver ponds, and small lakes. Occasionally a moment of humour broke the tedium of the search effort. One officer found a large white fungus, known as artist's conch, and drew a map on it showing the location of the "treasure". Then he left it along the trail for other officers to find.*

*Besides Staff Sergeant Stan Palmateer (District Headquarters, Peterborough), the search team members from the OPP were: Const. George Mountsteven (Haliburton detachment); constables Don Lacombe, M. Nimigon, and S.J. Gray (Peterborough); Const. Charles Potier (Cobourg); Cpl. Ted Grubb (Whitby); Const. Martin Bundle (Perth); Const. J.R. Wilson (Pembroke); Cpl. Ted Lummis and Const. G. Oliver (Belleville); Const. Murray Joynt (Bowmanville). Robert McGeachie of Coe Hill acted as official guide. During the five-week search, the squad was billeted at the River Bend Motel in Bancroft.

After the suspects were safely lodged in jail, French-speaking OPP Constable Jules Blouin, a native of Sault Ste. Marie, was planted in an adjoining cell in the guise of a break-and-enter suspect. He spent part of the first day in Cell Block Four, with Yvon and Hermyle Lalonde and Martel, but was later transferred to Cell Block One where Jean Claude Lalonde and Roger Poirier were lodged. The suspects were all French speaking and it was hoped that the men would reveal in their conversation with each other where the money had been stashed.

But after two days in the cell blocks with the prisoners, his entire report was put down on only one page. He only recorded what he felt was incriminating. He also admitted that while he spoke French well he could not understand it as well as English. He recorded that most of the conversation had been in French but recalled that once when Lalonde and Poirier were pacing the floor, another prisoner remarked, "I thought you would have had enough walking in the bush." At this Lalonde got quite mad and told the other man that he could "outwalk you in the bush any time. I walked four days and four nights without sleep."

Constable Blouin also reported how Hermyle Lalonde had come into the cell and showed the other prisoners his sore feet. When he went out Yvon Lalonde remarked that he was his brother and had a bad heart. He did not hear the prisoners implicate themselves in the robbery nor reveal any clues to the whereabouts of the money.

Constable Claude Courveille of the Cobourg OPP detachment was also fluent in French. Again pretending to be a prisoner, he was put in the "bull pen" with the other prisoners.

The only conversations he heard clearly were when they got mad and came out with only skimpy snatches of conversation: Hermyle Lalonde and Martel to Yvon Lalonde: "... you should have been more careful, your footprints were found at the car," to which Lalonde replied, "I was also scared and in a hurry to get away into the bush." Martel to Hermyle: "You should have cut the tops off your boots like we did." There was no answer. Hermyle sat and drew a sketch map on a magazine and added, "When we got to the four corners you turned right, didn't you?" Others strenuously denied this but Hermyle was adamant that at the four corners they had turned right. Martel agreed that at the four corners they and turned right. Hermyle to Martel: "You were 15 miles from the car." Martel to Hermyle: "You were 10 miles from the car." Hermyle: "I was 40 to 50 miles from the car when I was pinched." Martel: "No wonder you have sore feet." Hermyle: "It was mostly my toe."

From these snippets one might conjecture that after Yvon was captured, the other four continued together to the "four corners", then disagreed about which way to go, Martel, Poirier and Jean Claude going one way and Hermyle another. The "four corners" could have been any one of several road or road/rail intersections along the Old Hastings Road or Highway 62 between Highway 620 and the Steenburg Lake Road. By road, they were all about 14 miles from the abandoned Chrysler when they were "pinched"—although they all no doubt walked considerably farther as a result of having to keep to the bush much of the time.

Other snatches of conversation were accusations like "You should have stayed on the railroad tracks" and "I still had my jacket on … Don't worry about me. I know the bush and I know the place. I always look down when I am walking."

The *Peterborough Examiner* reported on September 12 that "the five men charged last week with armed robbery heard several more charges read against them in Peterborough magistrate's court today. Four of them today were charged with shooting with intent to wound while resisting arrest. This was in connection with shots that were fired at the police cruiser at the Crowe River bridge the day of the bank robbery. The same four have been charged with theft of the Buick and all five with theft of a 1961 Chrysler sedan which was abandoned after it blew two tires." In addition, Hermyle Lalonde was charged with breaking and entering a cottage on Bass Lake near Steenburg, belonging to Herb Hiles of Belleville.

Magistrate W.R. Philp remanded the men without plea on all charges pending a preliminary hearing to determine if the case should go to trial.

Three weeks after the suspects had been captured, some important new evidence came to light suggesting an aspect of the robbery plan which previously the police had not been aware of. On September 22, Edward McLean, a Detlor-area farmer, discovered the 1961 Oldsmobile car the robbers had hidden. It was parked in dense bush on his property, located east of Highway 62 about seven miles south of Bancroft. It had a Quebec licence plate. Close to it were signs of a campsite—hay strewn on the ground, some empty cans, cigarette packets, wrappers of food, etc. McLean reported his discovery to the OPP in Bancroft. The subsequent investigation linked the abandoned car to the suspects who were already in jail. Three wallets were found in the glove compartment. In one, there were cards made out to Roger Poirier and a YMCA card in the name of Roger Binnette. The second contained a Quebec chauffeur's licence made out to Marcel Lemieux. In the third was a licence made out to Claude Lemieux, some time payment cards from finance companies, and two "In Memorium" cards, one in memory of Eduoard Lalonde, the other illegible. The name Lemieux was an already-admitted alias of the Lalonde brothers.

The glove compartment of the Oldsmobile also yielded a plastic folder with a licence and ownership papers in the name of Lise Amyot, of 8th Avenue, Rosemount, Montreal. This address was the same as one taken from Yvon Lalonde at the time of his arrest. Other articles found by the officers were two walkie-talkie radios, a gun-cleaning outfit, a large box of fishing tackle, a grocery bill, a quantity of groceries, a magazine, a can opener, a road map of Calgary, knives, spoons, forks, dishes, camp stove and a lantern. A rack on top of the car held five sleeping bags. Corporal Bill Baluk was called to gather evidence and to dust for fingerprints, but as with the other two cars, found none.

On October 3, when the preliminary hearing began, nearly 100 bystanders were waiting outside the Peterborough County Courthouse to see the five men brought from the Whitby jail in two OPP cars. They were dressed in neat suits, two of them with ties and handkerchiefs in their breast pockets. A conversation was overheard in the courthouse corridor when some spectators remarked that "they don't look like criminals, I hope they get off."

A lad about 15 years old was spotted in the passage trying to slip something into the hand of one of the prisoners. An alert constable grabbed him, hustled him into a side room and searched him from his ducktail haircut to the toes of his grubby, pointed Wellington boots. Inspector Larry Gartner quizzed the boy and then consulted with Crown Attorney John Bradshaw. He had been trying to smuggle his "heroes" a packet of tobacco. The lad was allowed to go with a severe dressing down.

Just before the hearing began, as the prisoners were about to be escorted to the prisoners' bench, Hermyle Lalonde clutched his chest and called out that he needed his pills. His medication had been taken away from him and locked in a cupboard. But he was dead before the nitro-glycerine pills were located and rushed to him. The start of the preliminary hearing was postponed to the following day.

On this day that Hermyle died, the police publicly revealed his real name was Hermyle Lalonde, 36, of Montreal, brother of Yvon and Jean Claude Lalonde. Raymond Daoust, one of three defence lawyers acting for the accused (and who translated into French for the benefit of the prisoners), said in a statement issued to the press that Hermyle's doctor in Montreal had warned him never to be without nitro-glycerine pills in case of a heart attack. He also expressed the opinion that Ontario Attorney General Kelso Roberts should investigate the apparent culpable negligence that led to the death of the prisoner.

Hermyle Lalonde suffered from angina. In a statement, Daoust said, "On the evening before his death, I talked to Lalonde in jail. He complained that his medicine, on order of the jailer or the police, had been placed beyond his reach in a locked cupboard. I was going to protest about this the

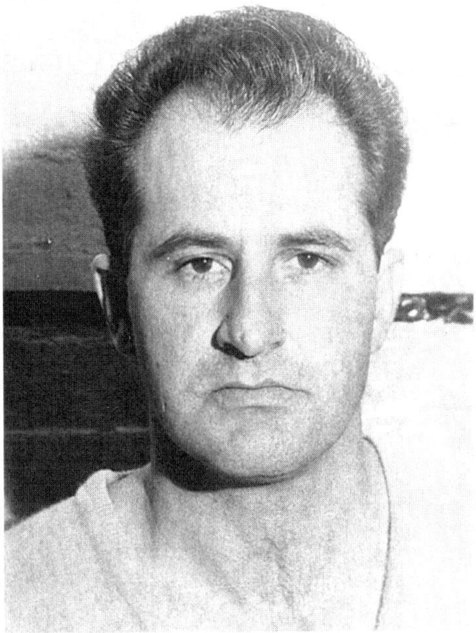

Hermyle Lalonde. *OPP Files*

next day when I learned of his sudden death ... I feel that a complete and impartial investigation should be held into all aspects of this tragedy." Attorney General Kelso Roberts said he had no comment on Mr. Daoust's statement, and that he would have to wait for a report before commenting.

On the same day, under the direction of the coroner, Dr. A. McNeill, an autopsy was performed by Dr. H.B. Wyatt, the assistant pathologist. Wyatt said that the pills had been taken from the prisoner on his arrest and said that it was routine not to allow a prisoner to have pills in his cell. He believed that the guard ran as fast as possible to get the pills.

At the end of the investigation the coroner ruled that the prisoner had died immediately from the heart attack and the pills would not have saved him. His heart had exploded and he was dead by the time he hit the floor. He remarked that on examination it was found that Hermyle had the heart of a 70-year-old due to his fast-paced lifestyle and that the heart showed scars from previous attacks. A tattoo on his arm read "Death before Dishonour". Scars told the story of his recovery from two bullet holes, inches apart in his back. They had both missed his spine and other vital areas. It was said that one bullet came from the gun of a bank clerk during a hold-up in Montreal; that one had knocked him to the ground. The second bullet was fired by a member of his own gang as he lay there while the others fled. It was suggested that an inquest should be held to investigate the circumstances of Hermyle Lalonde's death, but in court the defence lawyers accepted the verdict of the coroner.

No doubt the added stress of the most recent robbery and the four-day trek through the woods trying to elude the police had further weakened Hermyle Lalonde's heart.

When the preliminary hearing got under way on Wednesday, a chauffeur's licence was exhibited which gave Hermyle's address as 91151 24th Avenue, Ville St. Michel—a Montreal suburb. A phone call was made to the wife of this man. She responded by suggesting they should get in touch with his girlfriend. Three attractive young women had been seen in the area with the suspects before the robbery, and they were attending the hearings as spectators.

A camp operator just south of Bancroft testified at the preliminary trial. William Turpin of Islington operated a trailer park just south of Bancroft. He told how Yvon Lalonde had driven into his camp on the evening of August 28th in an Oldsmobile car. The Quebec licence number he had recorded matched the one found on the Oldsmobile found near Detlor. When Yvon arrived he had asked about the fishing in the area. He was the only guest at the camp that rainy night. Around midnight another car had driven in and had gone directly to the campsite where Yvon had parked. Mr. Turpin told how he had gone to bed and when he heard the second car arrive he presumed it was another guest. He had gotten up but by this time the second car and Yvon's had both driven away. However, Yvon was back the next morning. He had given his name as Perrie. Lalonde left the camp about 11 a.m. and drove south.

All this new evidence suggested that the robbers had set up a hidden camp where they could hide out for several days until the heat of a chase died down.

The purpose of the preliminary hearing was not to determine if the accused were guilty or not, but to see if there was enough evidence to warrant a full trial on the charges. The Crown didn't present all of its evidence here—just enough to convince the Court that the case should go to trial. Also testifying at the preliminary hearing were various police officers who had been involved in the chase, the search, and collecting evidence up to this point, as well as the bank manager and various witnesses who had seen the robbers prior to the crime and afterwards. Much of this testimony would be repeated at the trial itself if Magistrate Philp decided the case should proceed to that stage.

Not surprisingly, Magistrate Philp did order the surviv-

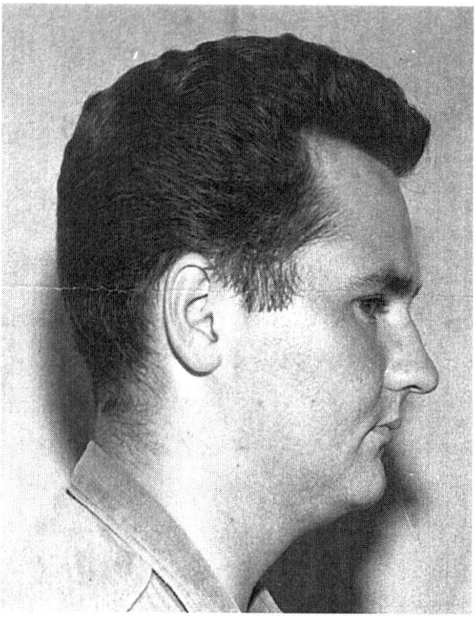

Jean Claude Lalonde was released on bail. *OPP Files*

ing four accused men to stand trial. In the meantime, the four would remain in custody at the Whitby jail. Arrangements would have to be made for a judge to rule over the trial. More evidence would have to be gathered. Crown Attorney John Bradshaw was selected to prosecute on behalf of the Crown. Witnesses would have to be subpoenaed to give evidence. Police officers who had played a role in the capture of the suspects would be called on to give their evidence. Specimens that had been gathered to provide concrete evidence at the trial would need to be documented and given numbers to provide easy reference during the trial. Dates for the court proceedings would have to be booked with the courthouse.

A date in December to start the trial was discussed, but the arrangements did not work.

For some obscure reason, in mid-December the decree came down that Jean Claude Lalonde would be released on bail of $30,000. He was the youngest of the prisoners and the only one who had not served a previous jail sentence. The large amount of bail money came from some unknown source and Jean Claude was once again allowed his freedom.

The other three prisoners continued to languish in the Whitby jail. As this was a modern detention centre, it is assumed they were not too uncomfortable. After their gruelling ordeal in the bush country back of Havelock, this accommodation was tolerable. Not luxurious, but not all bad. There were no swarms of mosquitoes to torment them, and while the bunks were not equipped with the best mattresses in the world, they beat sleeping out on the ground in a torrential rain. Their sore feet would have a chance to heal. As they sat in their cells and went over the events of the robbery and attempted getaway in their minds, it must have put their blood pressure up a few points to recall all the small bits of bad luck that had led to their eventual capture.

Meanwhile, in these not so uncomfortable surroundings, they planned strategy with their defence lawyers. John Mirsky, QC, from Ottawa, a renowned criminal lawyer, had been retained to defend the two Lalonde brothers, Yvon and Jean Claude. Another noted criminal lawyer, Arthur Maloney, QC, from Toronto, would handle the case for Poirier and Martel. The robbers were sure these high-priced lawyers would get them off. Yvon, who had not even been at the bank when the robbery took place, was confident that he would not be convicted. The others had all worn balaclavas: they could not be identified by witnesses at the scene of the robbery. And they had all worn gloves, too: there were no fingerprints in the bank or any of the cars. When they were captured, they did not have their masks, guns, gloves or any of the stolen money. The Crown would have to build its case against them entirely on circumstantial evidence. Convictions would be difficult to obtain, especially on the serious charges they faced.

The Trial

The trial of the four men charged with the armed robbery of the Toronto-Dominion Bank at Havelock on August 31, 1961, began on Monday, January 22, 1962. It ran for six days, through to Saturday, then recessed until Thursday, March 1, with testimony and closing arguments finally ending on Saturday, March 3—nine court days in all.

Prosecuting for the Crown was Crown Attorney John Bradshaw. John Mirsky, QC, and Arthur Maloney, QC, with Raymond Daoust assisting, were the counsel for the defendants. Judge A.R. Wilmott from Cobourg presided over the proceedings at the Peterborough County Courthouse. Also in attendance throughout, assisting the Crown Attorney, was

Laurence Gartner of the Criminal Investigations Branch. The OPP's chief investigator on the case, he was the person most familiar with all the evidence and the witnesses.

The four accused men pleaded "not guilty" to the charges against them. The charge of armed robbery read in court mentioned the sum of $230,000 that had not been recovered. Poirier, Martel and Jean Claude Lalonde also pleaded "not guilty" to four additional charges. Two of these involved possession of stolen autos, one of breaking and entering a summer cottage with intent, and the fourth, resisting arrest by shooting at OPP officer Jack McKendry

Poirier, Martel, and Yvon Lalonde appeared in court in custody. Jean Claude Lalonde, out on $30,000 bail since mid-December, was also in attendance. Judge Wilmott refused a request by the Crown that the bail now be cancelled. Defence lawyer Mirsky, acting for the Lalonde brothers, had opposed the request. Mr. Bradshaw explained that it was a matter of convenience. Jean Claude would have to be searched each time he entered the courtroom. Mr. Mirsky said that his client did not mind the inconvenience.

It was expected that 50 prosecution witnesses would be called and about 100 exhibits entered as evidence. At the request of the defence counsel, the witnesses were excluded when the hearing began. These included police officers who would tell of their encounters with the accused and describe the evidence they'd found, as well as bank employees and civilians who had witnessed the robbery, the getaway, and other details pertinent to the case, or who had seen the accused prior to the robbery. After each witness testified, the defence would have the opportunity to cross-examine him or her, hoping to discredit evidence damaging to their clients or providing alternate interpretations of it.

The first witness was John Pierce, a land surveyor, who provided maps and photographs that had been taken at the request of the police. He also presented a sketch he had made of the floorplan of the bank where the robbery had occurred.

The second witness was OPP identification officer Corporal Bill Baluk of Cobourg. He produced a series of photographs taken by him on the day of the robbery and on subsequent days. These included shots of the robbers at the time of their arrest as well as close-ups of footprints and views of the Buick and the Chrysler abandoned north of Havelock. A gunny sack found in the Buick, which contained 154 rounds of M1 carbine ammunition and 24 rounds of .38-special revolver ammunition, was one of the exhibits. It had been discovered by Baluk as he combed through the Buick looking for evidence that would link the suspects to the crime scene. These and other exhibits were turned over to the Attorney General's crime laboratory. Corporal Baluk identified several pairs of rubber boots removed from the accused men following their arrest. He noted that the sole designs of three pairs were identical. Boots taken from Hermyle Lalonde had a sole design that differed from the others. Clothing taken from Hermyle was identified by Baluk.

Corporal Baluk showed the photograph of the 1961 Oldsmobile discovered almost a month after the robbery in a laneway off a side road, about seven miles south of Bancroft. Near the car, he said, he found evidence that a tent had been pitched and canned goods consumed.

Baluk said he searched the bank on the day of the rob-

Corporal Bill Baluk, based at the Cobourg OPP detachment, was Criminal Identification Officer for District 8. *Bill Baluk*

bery. On the way down to the basement he found a flashlight and a pair of pliers. To Mr. Mirsky, Baluk replied that he had not found any fingerprints anywhere at the bank nor on the abandoned cars.

On the second day of the trial the first witness was Minnie Williams, who operated a gift and hobby shop and lived across the street from the bank. Miss Williams recalled getting up at 4 a.m. Looking out the window to the street, she saw a green car parked in the driveway of the house across the street. Her sister lived in this house and she thought it strange to see a car she did not recognize parked there. As she was eating her breakfast in the morning she heard the roar of a car motor starting up and saw two hooded men jumping into the car which then roared off to the west.

Miss Williams identified Roger Poirier as one of the men who had been in her store a couple of days before the robbery. She said the men spoke in a language other than English and she did not know what they talked about. When she pointed to Poirier and identified him as one of the men in her store, the defence counsel questioned her about her vision. She said she also recognized him by his posture and that she had no hesitation in picking him out. She replied that she wore glasses but her eyesight with them was good. At the preliminary trial she had also identified Hermyle Lalonde as having been in her store with Poirier. When he asked why she was up at 4 a.m. looking out the window, the defence lawyer wondered if she were a "village fire-watcher." She replied, "I suppose so."

George Milliken, the bank manager, testified at this court session too. He described the actions of himself and his staff preceding the robbery, and the details of the hold-up itself. The hold-up occurred about 9:15 a.m. "The first thing I knew was a noise at the west entrance," said the manager. "I saw nothing until a hooded man pointed a gun across my desk at me and told me to do what I was told." The man had a French-Canadian accent. He ordered the manager out of his office. At the same time, three masked men were giving orders to the other bank staff. The balaclavas they wore were khaki coloured and were knitted. Three of the men wore navy blue car coats. All wore leather gloves and blue jeans rolled up. Beneath these he could see rubber boots. One wore a blue-grey windbreaker. The man who held the manager at bay had a revolver. Two of the other men had revolvers and the third a rifle that looked like a cut-down .22.

Mr. Bradshaw showed Milliken an M1 carbine. This exhibit had been loaned by the military to identify the kind of weapon. The bandit weapon had never been recovered. The witness said this weapon was somewhat larger than the one he saw in the bank.

The smallest of the men, who carried the rifle, took charge and told the staff that no one would be harmed if they did what they were told. This man had no accent. "He was a Canadian." Meanwhile, two other men were cleaning out the tills and one man threatened to shoot. "He seemed quite anxious to shoot," Milliken said. This man had a French-Canadian accent. "At the start I was very frightened but I regained my composure and started to help the staff." Two of the men entered the vault after the manager opened it and emptied the cash and securities from the safe. All the staff was then ordered into the vault and the door clanged shut. Mr. Milliken said he was able to open the vault from the inside within a minute or two. He saw that the rear entrance of the bank was open and the robbers were gone. After checking his own phone and finding it dead he ran out to a store to call police.

Mr. Milliken gave a breakdown of the cash and documents taken: $84,499.98 in cash, $105,350 in bonds, $38,712 in stocks, and $3,640 in traveller's cheques. Total: $232,201.98.

It was discovered after the robbery that a basement window at the rear of the building had been jimmied open. The manager also mentioned finding a pair of pliers in the basement after the robbery.

Bank accountant James Bush said the rubber boots taken from the accused looked pretty similar to the ones worn by the bandits. They were olive drab with yellow soles. He said the carbine was similar to the one used by the hold-up men except that the stock was darker wood.

The trial dragged on. Much of the evidence was routine. Constable Milo Chapman testified, recalling picking up the woman on The Ridge Road. He identified Yvon as the driver of the car he met. He told of footprints leading away from the abandoned Chrysler. One set of footprints showed a pointed toe shoe, the other set a rubber boot print. The prints matched those from two of the exhibited sets of footwear taken from the robbers. Chapman had next seen Yvon in the boathouse after he had been captured and recognized him as the driver of the car because "of the face he has." Mr. Mirsky handed Chapman a photo taken after the arrest and asked him if he remembered the feather in Lalonde's hat. That was shown in the photograph. Chapman said he remembered it only to have Mirsky inform the Court that the feather was on the wall of the boathouse where the photo was taken. It was not a feather in Lalonde's hat nor was it a feather in Chapman's to be so tricked in giving evidence.

During testimony regarding the tracking down and capture of the suspects, the issue was raised of civilians having taken part in the search. Mr. Mirsky produced a copy of the *Peterborough Examiner* which showed a picture of Curtis Fitzgibbon brandishing a carbine. John Bradshaw objected and Mirsky replied that photographs don't lie. Judge Wilmott ruled that the questioning could proceed to a second picture showing Schultz and Shaw and Lalonde. Mr. Mirsky came back to questions about Curtis Fitzgibbon and Bradshaw once again objected, saying that the information regarding his presence was taken from a newspaper caption and should not be admitted.

Each day of the trial, spectators crowded the courtroom. The proceedings had become a high-interest drama unfolding before the eyes of those who attended. Only those spectators who could be seated were allowed in the courtroom and at some sessions would-be onlookers were turned away. It took on the atmosphere of a small live-theatre production. In the dead of winter in Peterborough, where could one find better entertainment? At one point while the legal counsel was conducting a cross-examination of a witness, a voice had come from the audience, yelling "Liar." The spectators in the courtroom were kept entertained—and admission had been free!

But if the spectators were amused, the Crown Attorney, the Judge, and lawyers who were defending the accused were deadly earnest. The serious business of finding enough circumstantial evidence to prove the suspects guilty of the crime was a grindingly slow affair. As the Crown presented more evidence, John Mirsky, QC, defendant for the two Lalonde brothers, said he was prepared to concede that Yvon and Jean Claude Lalonde were also known by the names Jean Claude and Yvon Lemieux.

Jean Claude Lalonde was still out on bail. On the fifth day of the trial he arrived in a pink taxi accompanied by four defence lawyers. He entered the courthouse clutching several law books. Each time he entered the courthouse he was searched. Was he enjoying the grand entrance that he made upon his arrival? At the young age of 24 the attention he was granted must have built up his ego. Throughout the trial to this point, the suspects had appeared calm, almost nonchalant.

On one trial day, a blonde woman spectator was pointed out in the audience by witness Charles Lummiss, who lived near the Crowe River bridge. He testified to having seen her in the area with Martel. She had come to his house back in July 1961 enquiring about the location of a lot that was for sale in Methuen Township. Mr. Lummiss said he did not know the woman's name, but Crown Attorney John Bradshaw identified the woman as Lise Amyot. Mr. Lummiss said the man he took to be Roger Martel stood some 50 yards away, beside a car parked on the road, while the woman made her enquiry. The blonde woman was one of three attractive young women—a blonde, a brunette and a redhead—who had been present during the week's hearings and had also turned up at several of the earlier hearings. Mr. Lummiss also testified that the deceased, Hermyle Lalonde, had also stopped at his house in June to enquire if he knew anything about some lots that were for sale in the Bass Lake area.

Interestingly, Lise Amyot and her attractive female companions were absent from the courtroom on the next trial day.

Constable George Mountsteven of the Haliburton OPP detachment testified. He verified photographs that had been entered as exhibits. One showed a small hunt camp in Limerick Township about four miles north of Murphy Corners (this would be a little south of Ormsby, and east of the Old Hastings Road). Others showed photographs of sections of the interior of the cottage and its surroundings. Mr. Maloney interrupted the testimony, charging that "this evidence was remote." Judge Wilmott ruled that he would let the evidence stand and allow Mountsteven to proceed.

Constable Mountsteven then described how the south window of the cottage had been forced. He commented on photographs that showed boot prints on a table bench under the window. He told Mr. Mirsky that he had taken a three-year course in criminal identification but that he was unable to be positive as to how long the footprints had been there. He identified pictures of three pairs of boot tops found under a spruce tree 85 paces from the cottage. These were later matched up with the rubber boots the fugitives had been wearing when they were captured. The design on the soles of the rubbers the men had worn had a similar tread pattern. All of these articles were on exhibit. After Maloney had protested the Crown's "little bits and pieces of evidence," Judge Wilmott said he would reserve his decision on whether the photographs objected to should be stricken from the record. Mr. Maloney said that the Crown was trying to enter as evidence "everything but the kitchen sink."

Sergeant Stan Palmateer, who had directed the ground search, testified that he had seen several sets of footprints on a road close to where the disabled Chrysler was found. He said the tracks had been followed for a distance of 29 miles. Finally, one set with broad bars left the others and turned east. Three sets of tracks, similar to the three pairs of boots on exhibit, continued north. He followed these tracks to the CNR line. Near Highway 62 he observed at least one man on the railway. Then he saw two men running into the bush. Some officers and civilian volunteers went into the bush and later returned with Jean Claude Lalonde, Poirier and Martel. On viewing the prisoners, Palmateer noted there was a considerable change in Martel's appearance since his imprisonment. His hair had a definite red hue at the time of his arrest. Mr. Bradshaw noted at this point that an earlier witness had said he remembered Martel's hair as being much darker.

When asked about the photograph that had appeared in the *Peterborough Examiner* showing the crowd scene following the arrest of the men, Palmateer said not everyone shown in the picture had participated in the search. Mr. Mirsky remarked, "Didn't everyone including the Boy Scouts want to search for the Treasure?"

Other evidence revealed by Palmateer in his court appearance was his identification of items that were on exhibit: a pair of overalls and a smock that had been found under the low-lying branches of a spruce tree on the trail. He also identified a shoulder holster that had been found on the trail across to The Ridge Road.

As the trial continued, a piece of evidence that would prove controversial was introduced. When Bill Baluk, the fingerprint expert, dusted the bank, he found no fingerprints, but he did find other bits of evidence. He had vacuumed up some dust from the basement and sent it off to the crime lab to see if it would match dust from the prisoners' clothes. The clothing stripped from the prisoners when they were captured had all been parcelled up with great care and sent off to the lab for scrutiny. At the lab, as the articles of clothing were being shaken out, particles of blue plastic had been discovered. These presumably came from the handles of the pliers found in the bank basement. It was assumed that these were the pliers used to cut the telephone and burglar alarm wires. The Crown hoped these particles would forge the link between the suspects and the scene. The defence had argued that the pliers were just like any other pair that could be bought at a Canadian Tire store. But instead of having these small blue particles displayed as an exhibit which could be examined as evidence, the Court heard how they had been "destroyed" during tests at the Attorney General's laboratory.

Mr. Bradshaw's announcement, made after he consulted with two laboratory experts, brought Arthur Maloney, QC, to his feet: "I never heard of such a thing. Two bits of evidence are thrown at us and then they have disappeared." Mr. Bradshaw responded, "No, not disappeared—burnt up." Mr. Maloney said he would submit that "the scientific evidence that is no longer evident is probably inadmissible anyway." Bradshaw objected to the term "destroyed". He said that they had been "consumed" during testing. Mr. Maloney preferred the term "obliterated". He submitted that crime officials had no right to proceed with the tests, knowing that the particles might possibly be destroyed in the process, without consulting the defence beforehand. Maloney said the law on this point—the right of the defence to examine and test exhibits—was so mandatory that the laboratory would be held in contempt of court if it refused to release the exhibits. These small particles that had been submitted for testing were just not available for examination. They had "burned up."

After this sparring between the Crown and the defence, Norman Erickson, a crime laboratory analyst, testified. He told how the various exhibits were examined after being received from the police. The articles of clothing were shaken out and the shakings were then put through a sieving process.

Mr. Clair, also from the laboratory, produced a small transparent box containing some remaining minute particles of the substance that had been "obliterated in the lab." The similarity of the material had been established by x-ray, he reported, and also by infrared spectrophotometer. The only conclusion that could be reached was that the materials were "not different" from the blue pliers found in the basement of the bank.

Mr. Clair also referred to particles of glass found in the clothing of two of the accused and in clothing found in the bush north of Havelock. He said the glass particles were similar to glass found in dust that had been scooped out of the back of the Buick getaway car. He said that he could not positively identify the particles as being from the Buick, whose rear window was shattered during the police chase. He admitted that he was not too familiar with the plate glass used in store windows or with auto glass.

This evidence from the crime lab was presented on Friday, the fifth day of the trial. So far 38 witnesses had been called and 58 exhibits entered. It had been hoped that the trial would have wound up at this point, but the Crown said it had 15 more witnesses to bring forth. This court session that was supposed to have ended on Friday was carried over until Saturday morning.

Constable Gordon Gray, of the Campbellford OPP detachment, testified on Saturday morning. As the village of Havelock was in the Campbellford OPP jurisdiction, the task of investigating the bank robbery fell initially in his lap. He recalled how he had been in his new post in Campbellford for just 15 minutes when the call came in reporting the bank hold-up in Havelock. The constable said he headed for Havelock, then went north along the Twin Lakes Road. There he came upon the abandoned Buick getaway car. Later he went to The Ridge Road and viewed the disabled Chrysler. He then walked west from the Chrysler along the "old west road" (the bush road). He recalled seeing marks in the grass which indicated that a car had been driven onto the grass and back out again. He measured the distance back to the Buick as 3¼ miles. He described footprints he discovered. They were made by boots with 13 ridges across the soles. He had counted the ridges in the mud. One print was different from three other sets. It had six bars across the soles. He estimated the footprints were several hours old.

Gray also testified to being in the boathouse where Yvon Lalonde was taken after his arrest. He took possession of a wallet containing cards and papers and a pair of sunglasses found on Lalonde. A fishing licence in the wallet had been purchased at Alfred, Ontario, a village in Prescott County near the Quebec border. The licence gave Lalonde's address as 5836 8th Avenue, Montreal. It was dated August 26—five days before the robbery.

At this stage in the trial, after six days of testimony, the defence lawyers sought an adjournment so that they could study the evidence—particularly the "obliterated" evidence—and attend to other important court matters. After Judge Wilmott consulted with the Crown, a tentative date of February 19 was mentioned for resumption of the trial. Crown Attorney Bradshaw assured the defence lawyers that they could speak with the crime lab people during the adjournment.

The trial did not resume, in fact, until March 1. Several more Crown witnesses testified, including the French-speaking officers who had been planted in the jail back in September to eavesdrop on the prisoners. Defence lawyer Maloney suggested that their testimony was "incomplete, imperfect and imprecise," but Judge Wilmott refused to strike it from the record. When a comment was made in French about the status of the planted officers, the Judge said that in English they were called "stool pigeons," prompting a ripple of laughter in the courtroom.

The final Crown witness was Inspector Laurence Gartner, of the OPP's Criminal Investigation Branch. The CIB had been called in to oversee this case. This was a routine procedure for all major criminal investigations. Gartner had been on the case from day one as the search was conducted for the suspects. He had gathered all the evidence that was to be presented at the trial and prepared all the exhibits. He had lined up all the witnesses who had played a role in this drama to tell their individual stories. He had attended every court hearing.

Inspector Gartner told of the search that had been carried out and of seeing Yvon Lalonde for the first time in the boathouse shortly after his arrest. At that time, Lalonde had protested that "I don't know what you want with me. I was just hitch-hiking and I got lost." When Lalonde was searched, a key ring with three keys was found. He described how he tried one of these keys in the Buick getaway car and found that it started the motor. Another key started the Chrysler motor and the third key activated the motor of the Oldsmobile found three weeks after the robbery in the farm field near Detlor. Gartner also said that he understood it to be true that the keys of some General Motors cars fitted other General Motors products.

Gartner had also seen Poirier, Martel and Jean Claude Lalonde after they had been brought in at Millbridge. This trio upon questioning said they had been "prospecting" and denied any knowledge of the robbery. He also saw Hermyle Lalonde in a police cruiser after he had been picked up. He appeared to be suffering from a heart problem and was given some pills he carried. He then recovered but suffered a fatal heart attack later while the preliminary trial was being carried out in October.

He said that an attempt had been made to make a plaster cast of the footprints but this had proved unsuccessful.

Mr. Mirsky, defence lawyer for the Lalonde brothers, made his closing arguments. He remarked that no fingerprints had been found at the bank. He said that it was possible that whoever held up the bank and escaped in the Buick had rendezvoused with another car and made good their escape. He pointed out that it was several hours before police roadblocks were set up around the entire area. He used a topographical map to point out several avenues of escape and said there was no evidence to discount this theory. He stressed that none of the accused had been found with any stolen money or clothing that would connect them to the robbery.

Dealing with the charge of resisting arrest by shooting—a charge faced by all except Yvon—he said the men clearly had an opportunity to shoot an officer with an automatic at a

Deputy Commissioner Laurence Gartner. While an Inspector with the CIB, he directed the Havelock bank robbery investigation. *L. Gartner*

distance of 40 feet but this was not done. The officers, he said, had agreed when giving their evidence that the shots went wild. It had not been established that the man with the gun had intended to shoot the officer. Mr. Mirsky also reminded the Court of the terrible hazard of unsure identification.

Mr. Bradshaw interrupted the defence lawyer to enquire why these men were running away if they were only on fishing trip or just lost. Mr. Mirsky recalled that there had been several cottage break-ins in the area and that it was possible the accused men were trying to run away as a result of these break-ins.

In his remarks, Mr. Mirsky also pointed out that not a single witness had stated clearly that any footprints found in the search area had been made by the rubber boots that were exhibited in Court. These were the boots that had been taken from the accused when they were apprehended. It was possible, he said that the clients were in the area in "slightly suspicious circumstances" but no proof had been offered that they were other than men on a fishing trip. Judge Wilmott intercepted to remark that he could not accept that these men were "just on a fishing trip." He could see no reason for breaking into cottages unless there was some motive.

When Mr. Mirsky dealt with the Oldsmobile that had been found three weeks later, he admitted that Yvon Lalonde had been the driver of this car, but for some time after he was seen in the car he had been in custody. He said that it was possible his clients were trying to evade the police as a result of the cottage break-ins. The defence lawyer ruled out the evidence given by the two bilingual officers who had eavesdropped on the accused in the jail. He also maintained that it had not been proven that Yvon Lalonde had any connection to the bank robbery.

Arthur Maloney, defending Martel and Poirier, delivered a long discourse on behalf of his clients. His strongest point was that none of the guns or the bulky clothing worn by the robbers at the bank scene had been recovered. He said the rubber boots worn by the accused may have linked them to footprints found in the bush, but not to the scene of the robbery. He emphasized that the loot from the bank had not been found despite a lengthy search of the area. Judge Wilmott intervened to comment that the 30-square-mile search area also contained a good deal of water.

Maloney also maintained there was a "plausible possibility" that two or more of the men left the Buick before it was abandoned. If this were so, "it put all kinds of holes in the Crown case."

Mr. Maloney submitted that the large amount of food and the fishing tackle found at the Oldsmobile in the farm field, gave strong evidence of the reason that the men were in the area. He told the Court that if there was a single fact that was consistent with guilt, it must also be inconsistent with innocence. He asked for a dismissal on all counts against his clients.

Crown Attorney Bradshaw gave his summation. He said that there were no fingerprints at the bank because the robbers wore gloves and that there also were not any positive identification of the suspects because they wore balaclavas. But, there was a mass of circumstantial evidence. The Crown's theory was that Yvon Lalonde was never at the bank. In order to convict him he had to argue that he was a party to what the others did. He submitted that there was a pre-conceived plan in which Yvon was one of the conspirators. He added that the men had not been charged with conspiracy and he would ask the Court to consider this now. It was evident that the robbery was well planned. One proof of this was the Oldsmobile that had been seen several days before the robbery in the Bancroft area and was found later in the bush. He drew attention to the manner in which the severing of the telephone lines at the bank had been timed. The wires were cut only moments after a bank official had called in from outside to double check that all was well inside. Had these wires been cut five minutes earlier their would have been an alert. It appeared that the bank robbers were in the basement all night.

After Mr. Bradshaw's submission, Mr. Mirsky congratulated him and the police on their excellent presentation of the case. However, he said the case fell "far short of the evidence necessary for a conviction on circumstantial evidence." He said that even the Crown admitted that the evidence was circumstantial. The Court must take care, he said, not to convict anyone on suspicions only. He submitted that Yvon Lalonde had never been at the bank that had been robbed on the morning of August 31.

Court recessed for a few minutes while assistant defence counsel Raymond Daoust went through the records in French with the prisoners. The records showed that Jean Claude Lalonde, the youngest of the accused, had been convicted of armed robbery four years earlier. He had been given only a two-year suspended sentence for this offence and it was pointed out that the circumstances must have warranted such a lenient sentence. The other three accused, however, all had long records, including crimes of violence. It was revealed too that Roger Poirier had been on bail in Montreal, pending trial for attempted murder, at the time of the Havelock robbery. Crown Attorney Bradshaw asked for maximum penalties and reminded the Court that they could be given 20 years.

Mr. Maloney gave a speech stressing that all of the accused were products of the slums of Montreal. He said that history had shown that phrases such as "protection of the public" were outmoded and that new approaches to rehabilitation and reformation were paying off. He noted that of the accused, only Jean Claude had an education as high as Grade 9. The others left school much earlier and Martel could neither read nor write. All of the accused, he said, had indifferent work backgrounds, some being truck drivers and all of them at some time having been employed as bartenders or doormen. In every case he pleaded before the courts, one or more of a certain set of factors were found: poverty, broken homes, drunkenness, divorce, lack of opportunity and lack of education. Some of these factors appeared in the case of each of the accused. "Society," he said, "has a certain measure of guilt in the case of every individual who appears before the court. Steps are now being taken: slum removal projects, extension of probation services, and so forth to change the old system. In this new society long sentences are out of place. They will not really protect society." In further outlining the background of the accused men, Mr. Maloney said that Martel was the father of four children (aged 14, 12, 11 and 4) while Poirier had a 5-year-old son.

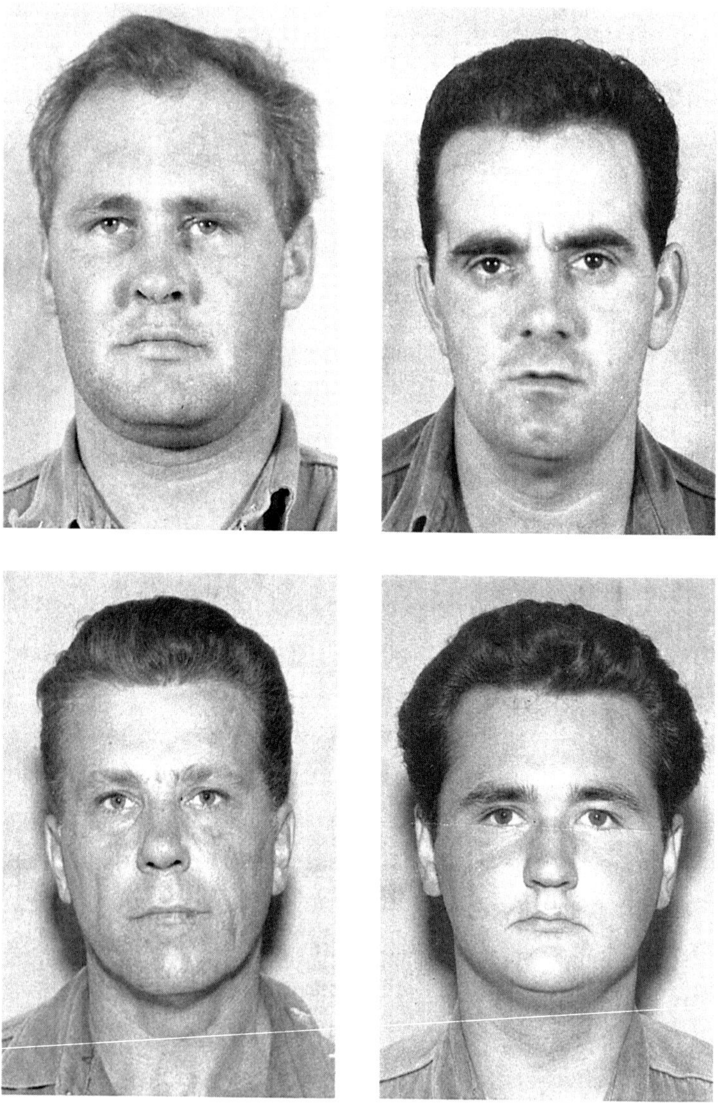

The four men who stood trial and were convicted for the armed robbery of the Havelock Toronto-Dominion Bank. Clockwise from upper left: Yvon Lalonde, Roger Poirier, Jean Claude Lalonde, and Roger Martel. The fifth gang member, Hermyle Lalonde, died prior to the trial. *OPP Files*

At the conclusion of the closing arguments on Saturday, March 3, Judge Wilmott indicated that he would likely hand down his verdict on Monday. At this point he ordered Jean Claude Lalonde back into custody.

Crown Attorney Bradshaw stated that whatever the outcome, the case might well stand as an authority on circumstantial evidence for many years to come.

At exactly 11:01 a.m. on Monday, Judge Wilmott entered a tense, packed courtroom and began to deliver his verdict. In the nearly two hours it took, he examined many aspects of the evidence. Although he noted that the evidence against the accused was all circumstantial, there was such an overwhelming amount of it that he could only reach one conclusion: guilt. Some particularly crucial evidence was the footprints left by the robbers: the pointed shoe marks, matching the shoes Yvon Lalonde was wearing when he was captured, appearing along with the rubber boot prints of the others, tied him in with the four who actually robbed the bank. Without that evidence, Judge Wilmott said he couldn't have found Yvon guilty. The judge also found persuasive the existence of the third car and the hidden camp south of Bancroft, which indicated a plan to hide away until the heat was off. He said that he was glad to be able to differentiate between Jean Claude and the others because of his youth and his brief record.

Judge Wilmott concluded his remarks with his pronouncement: "I find the four accused guilty on the first count in the indictment, namely—Guilty of Armed Robbery as charged." He handed Roger Martel, Roger Poirier and Yvon Lalonde 10-year prison terms, while Jean Claude Lalonde received a six-year sentence (the convictions were subsequently appealed, without success; the other, lesser charges faced by the men were dealt with later).

Throughout the trial the prisoners had appeared calm and were often smiling as Mr. Mirsky and Mr. Maloney knocked holes in the evidence being presented by the Crown. They appeared confident that the astute handling of the case by their lawyers would soon result in their freedom. But after Judge Wilmott made his declaration of guilt, the smiles quickly vanished as the prisoners were led away, handcuffed, to their cells. They were met briefly in the downstairs hall by the three attractive Montreal girls who earlier in the trial had made daily appearances in court. For a number of years now, the convicted men would have to content themselves with talking to them through a grille in a prison visiting room. Their new address was to be the Kingston Penitentiary.

Lawyer John Mirsky, who had unsuccessfully defended the Lalonde brothers, died a few days later as a result of a car crash in Montreal.

Conclusion

Success is simply a matter of Luck, ask any failure.

This is a quote by Earl Wilson.

The failure of this bold robbery can be attributed to some small unexpected delays or just to "bad luck". The group of professional thieves who carried out the caper could not have factored in all the variables that might possibly affect their split-second timing, and that prevented their meticulous plans from working out. It ended up like the report of the surgical procedure where "the operation was a success but the patient died."

Although the robbers were apprehended and incarcerated, the canvas sack of money was never located. Some people

..ave stated, "Oh, don't look for the money; it's been spent long ago." Could this be true? Did the robbers dig a hole ahead of time and just drop it in the hole as they fled? Is it in the bottom of Round Lake as I have been told? Or in one of the other lakes in the area? Is it buried deep in the earth where a metal detector cannot pick it up because the magnetic field is diverted by the rocks? Or in a swamp? Two milk cans were reported to have been stolen the night before the robbery. Do they contain the loot? Did the robbers pass the money on to the attractive sweater-clad girls who attended the trial and who were on hand to console them when they were sentenced? Was it taken out of the country. One rumour was that some of the bonds had been cashed in Switzerland. Could this be true? Was the loot just dropped right in Havelock for an accomplice to retrieve? A couple were stopped by police as they were travelling east on Highway 7 that morning. The car they were driving had a Quebec licence plate. When questioned, they produced a check-out voucher proving that they had stayed in the Royal York Hotel in Toronto the night before. Considering their check-out time in Toronto, it was possible they passed through Havelock at the very time of the robbery. Did they do a small detour off the main highway and pick up the loot on the way through to Montreal? Were they part of the plan?

Jean Claude Lalonde was the first of the four robbers out of prison. Released on parole in April 1966 after serving four years of his six-year sentence, he was sent back to his native Montreal. It was reported in the *Peterborough Examiner* on August 31, 1966—the fifth anniversary of the robbery—that while in prison, authorities had talked with Lalonde about a parole deal in exchange for telling where they'd hidden the loot. Police wouldn't confirm this. In any event, the whereabouts of the money remained a mystery. Jean Claude was kept under close surveillance for more than a month after his release, and a helicopter monitored the getaway route and search area. But he did not lead authorities to the missing loot.

The four prisoners had originally been put in the Kingston Penitentiary. However, as a result of disturbances early in their sentences, three of them were moved to other institutions. By 1966 Roger Poirier was on death row at the Dorchester Penitentiary in New Brunswick, having stabbed another inmate to death.

Five years after the robbery, the U.S. Fidelity and Guaranty Company of Toronto, the Toronto-Dominion Bank's insurance company, was still offering a 10 per cent reward for the safe return of all negotiable stocks, bonds and cash. A Fidelity investigator said the company was still working on the case "very strongly" and that all new leads were being checked out.

The haul from Havelock bank was believed to have been the largest in the recorded history of Ontario crime to that point.

Tempora utantor, et nos mutamur in illis.

Times change, and we change with them.

This quotation from Bartlett was adopted by the Ontario Provincial Police as their motto in 1969. Tremendous strides have been made in technological advancements that are now available to the Ontario police force. A canine search unit would have been a great asset at the time of the Havelock bank robbery. Instead of slogging through the bug-infested swamps and beating the bushes in all directions for five days, a good dog would most likely have sniffed out the trail of the robbers in a matter of hours. This was not an option at that time. Dogs were first used by the OPP in 1967 when Constable R.E. Carson was teamed up with "Cloud" at North Bay, while Constable C.V.E. Jones and "Arab" formed a crime-fighting duo in London, Ontario. There had been a rash of bank robberies in southwestern Ontario since 1965. Arab and his handler were credited with getting that situation under control.

There are many accounts of the role these specially trained dogs have played both in rescue and in the capture of dangerous suspects. One of the early success stories concerned a dog named "Butch". During a bank robbery investigation Butch led his master, P.C. Walker, through dense bush to recover $15,000 loot from a robbery and some guns that had been buried. In 1979 the Field Support Services Branch was expanded and included the Canine Search and Rescue teams under Superintendent John Gray. In 1981 the induction of the Purina Animal Hall of Fame Award gave recognition to some of the outstanding dogs in the team. A dog named "Lance" was the third dog to be so honoured. In the darkness he followed a trail for three hours to find a woman lost in the Mill Pond Conservation Area. The woman had become totally disoriented and was hopelessly tangled in underbrush. His master, Constable J.T. Murray, of Casselman, carried the exhausted woman back out through the wilderness trail with Lance leading the way. The return trip took more than two hours. Many of these early dogs had been trained by Abe Boley at Mount Forest. He prepared new dogs for the rigorous duties expected of them, and also conducted refresher courses for the dogs and their handlers on a regular basis.

In 1972 the OPP added two Bell Jet Ranger helicopters to their roster of equipment. Deputy Commissioner Gartner and Assistant Commissioner Loree went to Fort Worth, Texas, to take delivery of them. On their return the helicopters were based at the harbour in Toronto at the Great Lakes Helicopter facility. This advanced the capabilities of the force to assist in search and rescue operations as well as being available for emergency and disaster responses. Transportation of personnel was another role they were capable of accommodating.

Over the years the marine unit has expanded, giving the force the capability of monitoring activities on many small lakes. Many other updates in technology have provided safety features for the officers. Constables Morris Baker and Jack McKendry would have welcomed a bullet-proof vest back in 1961 at the Crowe River bridge. When these armoured vests were first brought into use for the force they were referred to as "second chance vests".

In this day of instant communication the use of cell phones is taken for granted. In 1961, officers depended upon receiving static-filled messages over a hand-held radio receiving unit in their cruiser. The messages were sent out from a central despatching office. On the first day of the search during the Havelock robbery operation, the radio control tower in Lakefield was inactive for one hour at one of the most crucial times. Walkie-talkies were used but they did not have a long range. Much of the communication during this manhunt was worked out by pre-arranged gunfire signals. Some of these were misinterpreted as actual gun battles.

Corporal Bill Baluk's camera equipment. When he retired, Bill traded the gear in for a set of golf clubs. *Bill Baluk*

Great strides have been made over the years in the field of forensic science in the testing of fibres, DNA testing and satellite monitoring. Cameras at that time were bulky and required a whole array of accompaniments in the way of extra film, light bulbs and lenses. In 1977 the OPP was the first police force in the world to purchase and put into operation an argon ion laser for the detection of fingerprint evidence. Electro-static detection apparatus was added to the field of crime detection aids.

Small banks, such as the bank at Havelock burglarized in 1961, are no longer easy targets. Surveillance cameras, motion detector devices and sensitive burglar alarm systems have provided protection. Brinks and other armoured trucks provide safe delivery of currency and other securities to banks. The Brinks company carries an all-risk insurance policy and employs armed guards. This has taken away much of the risk in delivery. And, as we move increasingly to a "cashless" society, the amount of cash money a bank needs to have on hand has been considerably reduced.

Working conditions for police officers has kept pace with the modern concept of employment. Officers now would not be expected to work a 36-hour straight shift. In those pre-union days they were allowed to bank hours that they could use for extra time off, in lieu of overtime pay—but only if it did not interfere with their regular work week, which was six days in summer and five days in winter.

After 45 years this story of the bank robbery in Havelock is still an unsolved mystery.

It is also a look back at the "way we were".

The Gut

During the Ice Age many thousands of years ago, the glaciers carved out "The Gut", a deep gorge in the Canadian Shield bedrock. Here the Crowe River flows through a fissure for about 700 feet. The fissure varies between 15 and 30 feet in width at the bottom and has a depth of over 100 feet. There is a waterfall just north of the chasm and the sounds of the water rushing over the falls and through this constrained channel is like listening to a great orchestral performance. All the high and low notes with the background of magical drums beating out a solid rhythm can be heard. From this location there is a breath-taking glimpse of the rugged terrain that surrounds it. The Gut, located 11 miles east of Apsley, lies within a 400-acre site purchased in 1976 by the Crowe Valley Conservation Authority. The site is now managed by the Ministry of Natural Resources and the Nature Conservancy of Canada.

The following story about a tragedy at The Gut was told to me by my friend Max. I include it here out of interest because it took place around the Crowe River bridge which figured so dramatically in the attempted getaway of the Havelock bank robbers.

The Story of The Gut

as told by Max

I was fishing on the Deer River about two miles from The Gut. Perhaps this would be back in 1950 or '51. Jim Wilson and I were using a 16-foot cedar-strip canvas-covered canoe. This canoe was freighter style. I casually mentioned that it seemed to be quite stable. Jim looked at me and shook his head. "Don't ever over-estimate a canoe or you'll find yourself in the water."

Nothing more was said for maybe five minutes and then he said, "I will tell you a story.

"As you know, I lived only a mile or so from here for several years in the late 1920s until the middle 1930s. What I'm going to tell you happened in 1930 or '31. These were the 'hungry thirties' and money was very scarce. Henry Bird, a neighbour, and I were trapping muskrats in the spring to try and make a few dollars.

"We put a canoe in the Crowe River about 50 yards upstream from the bridge. The river was very high with spring meltwater and there was some ice floating. Thinking of it now I realize we were foolish to be out on the river at that time of flood water, but we were both young and were very confident of our skills with a canoe.

"As we started up the river, we were hit by a water auger—a miniature whirlpool that sometimes develops in fast deep water where there are hidden obstructions. I don't think the canoe upset; I believe it threw us out as it spun. Whatever happened, we were in the water.

"We were wearing thigh-high rubber boots and these being full of air, the boots kept trying to float and stand me on my head. The shock of hitting that icy water had me gasping for breath and, of course, we were wearing heavy winter clothing, which was weighting me down. The first thing I had to do was get the boots full of water, so I could keep my head up. Henry disappeared and I never saw him alive again.

"As I went through under the bridge I tried to reach the girders, but failed. Of course I knew that I was in serious trouble and was going to need a lot of luck if I was to get out of this one. I tried to swim to shore but the current was so swift I couldn't make any headway, so I dropped to the bottom and crawled sideways on the river bottom. When I had to come up I was lucky to be in the lee of a big boulder and there was a clump of tag-alder brush near—the very last clump before the rapids. Had I gone into the rapids I would have drowned for sure. I grabbed the brush and pulled myself out on to the bank. I was so cold that I was stiff and paralyzed and I could not even stand up.

"Thoughts raced through my mind that I had to make it

The falls at The Gut. *Crowe Valley Conservation Authority*

to the Mission House, about a half mile away, or they would find me here on the bank like a frozen icicle. I crawled a short distance and finally got on my feet and started on a staggering run for the Mission. I fell many times but the farther I got the better I got. When I got out of the river I knew people were living in the Mission and the door would not be locked and there would be some wood heat in the stove, even if they were away. I made it, or I would not be sitting here telling you about it."

I asked him what happened to Henry.

"Well, the neighbours and I searched for several days. The authorities were not much involved. We found his body on an island down river a ways. He had been pulled down through that narrow 700-foot chasm with the force of the current. I went with a canoe and helped retrieve his mangled body."

I said that after his own narrow escape I thought he'd be afraid to go in a canoe.

His response was, "If I didn't go, I would never be able to set foot in one again."

Bibliography

Adams, Peter, and Colin Taylor, eds. *Peterborough and the Kawarthas*. Peterborough: Trent University Department of Geography, 1985.

Chapman, L.J., and D.F. Putnam. "Physiography of the South Central Portion of Southern Ontario." Map 2226, scale 1 inch to 4 miles. Toronto: Department of Mines and Northern Affairs, 1972.

———. "Physiography of the Georgian Bay–Ottawa Valley Area." Map 2228, scale 1 inch to 4 miles. Toronto: Ministry of Natural Resources, 1975.

Cole, A.O.C., ed. *Illustrated Historical Atlas of Peterborough*

County 1825–1875. Peterborough: Peterborough Historical Atlas Foundation Inc., 1975.

Galvin, Clare. *My Town, My Memories*. Ennismore [Ontario]: Prudence Felicity Publishing, 1993.

Hewitt, D.F. *Geology and Scenery: Peterborough–Bancroft–Madoc Area.* Geological Guide Book No. 3. Toronto: Ontario Department of Mines, 1969.

Higley, Dahn D. *The History of the Ontario Provincial Police Force*. Toronto: The Queen's Printer, 1984.

Hunter, Harold R. *The Township of Havelock Belmont Methuen.* Oshawa: Miracle Press, 2005.

———. *Havelock Through The Years*. Belleville: Mica Publishing, 1990.

"The Eclipse". Pamphlet. Rock and Rail Historical Festival, 1997.

Newspapers:

The Havelock Standard

Peterborough Examiner

Peterborough Review

Toronto Star

Index

Grace Barker received an Ontario Heritage Foundation award in 1999 for her work in preserving, protecting and promoting the rich heritage of the province. Her book *Timber Empire: The Exploits of the Entrepreneurial Boyds*, now in its second edition, traces the nineteenth-century adventures of Trent Valley lumber baron Mossom Boyd and his sons. In *The Bad Luck Bank Robbers*, she brings the reader a detailed account of another intriguing drama that had never been told. Grace now resides in Campbellford, Ontario. For more information about her books, please visit www.foxmeadowbooks.com.

AUTHOR PHOTO BY CORRIE ADAM